75 GREAT HIKES
MINNEAPOLIS
& ST. PAUL

JAKE KULJU

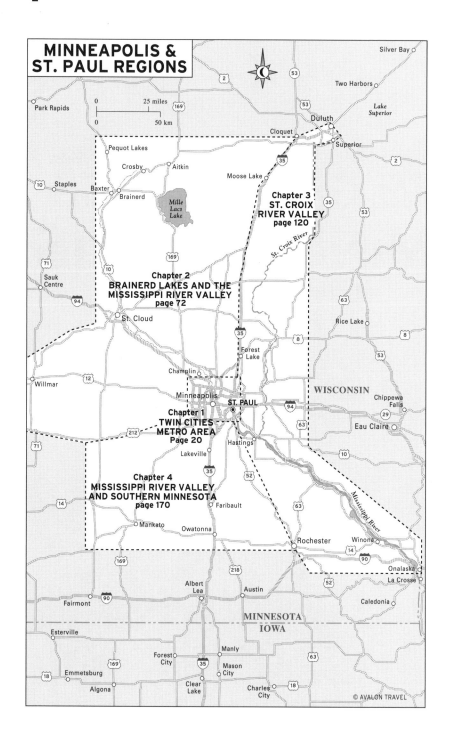

MINNEAPOLIS & ST. PAUL REGIONS

Silver Bay

Park Rapids

0   25 miles
0   50 km

Two Harbors

Lake Superior

Pequot Lakes

Crosby   Aitkin

Moose Lake

Duluth

Cloquet

Superior

Staples

Baxter   Brainerd

Mille Lacs Lake

**Chapter 3
ST. CROIX
RIVER VALLEY
page 120**

Sauk Centre

St. Croix River

**Chapter 2
BRAINERD LAKES AND THE
MISSISSIPPI RIVER VALLEY
page 72**

St. Cloud

Rice Lake

Forest Lake

Willmar

Champlin

Minneapolis

ST. PAUL

WISCONSIN

Chippewa Falls

**Chapter 1
TWIN CITIES
METRO AREA
Page 20**

Eau Claire

Hastings

Lakeville

**Chapter 4
MISSISSIPPI RIVER VALLEY
AND SOUTHERN MINNESOTA
page 170**

Faribault

Mankato   Owatonna

Rochester   Winona

Mississippi River

Onalaska

La Crosse

Albert Lea   Austin

Fairmont

Caledonia

**MINNESOTA
IOWA**

Esterville

Forest City

Manly

Emmetsburg

Mason City

Algona

Clear Lake

Charles City

© AVALON TRAVEL

Contents

How to Use This Book

ABOUT THE MAPS

This book is divided into chapters based on regions that are within close reach of the city; an overview map of these regions precedes the table of contents. Each chapter begins with a region map that shows the locations and numbers of the trails listed in that chapter.

Each trail profile is also accompanied by a detailed trail map that shows the hike route.

Map Symbols

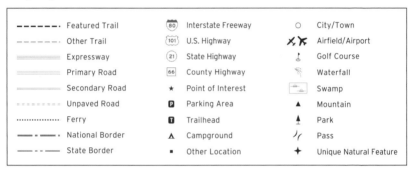

-------	Featured Trail	80	Interstate Freeway	○	City/Town
-------	Other Trail	101	U.S. Highway	✗✈	Airfield/Airport
≈≈≈≈≈	Expressway	21	State Highway	⚲	Golf Course
≈≈≈≈≈	Primary Road	66	County Highway	⚲	Waterfall
≈≈≈≈≈	Secondary Road	★	Point of Interest	≈	Swamp
=========	Unpaved Road	℗	Parking Area	▲	Mountain
....	Ferry	❶	Trailhead	⚑	Park
━━╺━━╸	National Border	▲	Campground	)ᵣ	Pass
━━╺╺━━	State Border	■	Other Location	✛	Unique Natural Feature

ABOUT THE TRAIL PROFILES

Each profile includes a narrative description of the trail's setting and terrain. This description also typically includes mile-by-mile hiking directions, as well as information about the trail's highlights and unique attributes.

The **mileage** and **elevation** for each hike as measured with a Garmin GPSMAP 64st. The elevation gain for each hike is cumulative; all the bumps and hills that you'll ascend throughout the hike are counted in the overall elevation gain.

In addition to the featured trail, each listing includes options on how to **shorten** or **lengthen** the hike, where to **hike nearby,** or how to extend the hike into a **day trip** or **get away for the weekend.**

Detailed driving **directions** are provided from the city center or from the intersection of major highways to the trailhead. GPS coordinates are included for the trailhead. When public transportation is available, instructions are noted after the directions.

ABOUT THE ICONS

The icons in this book are designed to provide at-a-glance information on special features for each trail.

The trail offers an opportunity for wildlife watching.

The trail features wildflower displays in spring.

The trail travels to a waterfall.

The trail visits a historic site.

Dogs are allowed.

The trail is appropriate for children.

The trail is wheelchair accessible.

The trailhead can be accessed via public transportation.

ABOUT THE DIFFICULTY RATING

Each profile includes a difficulty rating. Definitions for ratings follow. Remember that the difficulty level for any trail can change due to weather or trail conditions, so always phone ahead to check the current state of any trail.

Easy: Easy hikes are 4 miles or less and with an elevation gain or loss of 500 feet.

Easy/Moderate: Easy/Moderate hikes are 4–6 miles long and with an elevation gain or loss of 500–1,000 feet.

Moderate: Moderate hikes are 2–8 miles long and with an elevation gain or loss of 1,000–1,500 feet.

Strenuous: Strenuous hikes are 6–10 miles long and with an elevation gain or loss of 1,000–2,000 feet.

Butt-kicker: Butt-kicker hikes are 8–14 miles long with an elevation gain or loss of 2,000 feet or more.

INTRODUCTION

Author's Note

Because I'm from north-central Minnesota, my life has been framed around the outdoors since before I could tie my own hiking boots. Striding through majestic pine forests, swinging from gnarled oak branches, and swimming in north country rivers is what I do best.

Even though I was raised outside of the city, I've lived most of my adult life in the Twin Cities metro area. How do I cope? I've spent much of that time with my feet strapped into a pair of hiking boots, and I hardly let the dust settle on a trail before I come back for another visit.

St. Paul and Minneapolis boast more than 300 parks and open spaces with trail systems that total more than 200 miles. So despite living in a large metropolitan area, Twin Cities residents have their pick of places to get away from all the urban trappings.

Even though Minnesota's most well-known outdoor destinations are in the internationally renowned Boundary Waters Canoe Area Wilderness (BWCAW) and along Lake Superior and its rugged north shore, the areas within two hours of Minneapolis and St. Paul offer hikers some of the most scenic and peaceful trails in the country. The landscape, carved by the monolithic glaciers of the last ice age, is a mix of lakes, rivers, expansive wetlands, evergreen forests, and grassy prairies. The natural beauty of the region, combined with a sense of stewardship that prevails in Minnesotan culture, means that many areas around the state, and even within the Twin Cities themselves, are preserved as undeveloped parks with amazingly serene hiking areas.

If you like vast tallgrass prairies rife with blooming wildflowers, craggy cliffsides along rushing river ravines, and high blufftop overlooks with expansive vistas of the mighty Mississippi River, then you'll love the hikes in this book. From the rolling prairie lands of southwestern Minnesota to the major bird migratory corridor along the sloughs of the Minnesota River Valley south of the Twin Cities, a two-hour drive in any direction will reveal more peaceful natural spaces than you can shake a walking stick at. Try hopping over the glacial potholes along the St. Croix River Dalles. Climb the hundreds of wooden steps up the ravine walls along the Whitewater River. Watch a flock of hundreds of great blue heron come to nest in the cottonwood tree rookery just south of Minneapolis. You will come to view our great northern state in an entirely different light.

—Jake Kulju

Best Hikes

Can't decide where to hike this weekend? Try one of these unique hikes, grouped into some of my favorite categories.

Best Historical Hikes

St. Anthony Falls Heritage Trail and Pillsbury Islands, Twin Cities Metro Area, page 25

Mille Lacs Loop, Brainerd Lakes and the Mississippi River Valley, page 79

Grand Portage Trail, St. Croix River Valley, page 122

Pike Island Loop, Mississippi River Valley and Southern Minnesota, page 174

Sugar Camp Hollow and Big Spring Trail, Mississippi River Valley and Southern Minnesota, page 210

Best River Hikes

Two Bridges Loop, Twin Cities Metro Area, page 50

Crow Wing Confluence Trail, Brainerd Lakes and the Mississippi River Valley, page 74

Swinging Bridge and Summer Trail Loop, St. Croix River Valley, page 125

Quarry Loop to High Bluff Trail, St. Croix River Valley, page 132

Kinni Canyon Trail, St. Croix River Valley, page 149

Pike Island Loop, Mississippi River Valley and Southern Minnesota, page 174

Best for Viewing Wildlife

Crow Wing Confluence Trail, Brainerd Lakes and the Mississippi River Valley, page 74

Lake Rebecca Loop, Brainerd Lakes and the Mississippi River Valley, page 91

Swinging Bridge and Summer Trail Loop, St. Croix River Valley, page 125

Riverbend Trail, St. Croix River Valley, page 157

Big Woods Loop to Timber Doodle Trail, Mississippi River Valley and Southern Minnesota, page 198

Best Views

Crosby Farm Loop, Twin Cities Metro Area, page 56

Lake Pepin Overlook Hiking Club Trail, St. Croix River Valley, page 155

Hiking Tips

HIKING ESSENTIALS
Clothing
Minnesotans talk about the weather whenever they have the chance—and they often have the chance. A look out the window in the morning doesn't guarantee an accurate forecast for the afternoon. It is important to be prepared for changing weather conditions while out on the trail. Plan to dress in layers on cool days, wear moisture-wicking clothing in cold weather, and have adequate footwear for the terrain you will be walking on.

Three of Minnesota's four seasons have cool temperatures, and even summer nights can dip into the 40s. Fabrics like wool, polyester blends, and waterproof materials like Gore-Tex will help you be prepared for inclement weather. Wool is a naturally insulating fabric that will hold warmth even when it gets wet. Modern fabrics also combine insulating qualities, moisture wicking, and water resistance to keep you comfortable in the outdoors. Cotton fabrics absorb and hold moisture, and are not your best choice. If you plan on spending a lot of time on the trail, it is a good idea to spend some money on a few items of good clothing that will keep you comfortable.

Additionally, you should have a hat, a good pair of hiking boots that fit well, and a rain jacket or water-resistant jacket in your outdoor arsenal. On shorter hikes during the summer this may not always be necessary, but if rain strikes or the bugs get bad in the middle of the woods, having a head covering and a rain jacket can make the difference between a memorable storm encounter and a miserable and dangerous trudge back to the car.

Food and Water
Eat well, hike well. It's as simple as that. Aside from the discomfort of being hungry and thirsty while on the trail, not being prepared with food and water can be potentially dangerous. Carry what you need in a day pack, and focus on highly nutritious foods that don't take up a lot of space. Nuts, dried fruit, trail mix, and peanut butter are full of energy and easy to eat on the go. Bring a bottle of your own water or a filtration system. As a general guideline, you should plan to drink a little more than a cup of water per mile.

Navigational Tools
MAPS
A map is your best friend on the trail. In addition to saving you time and giving you more options, maps can prevent you from the embarrassing scenario of having to ask for directions. Parks often change their trail routes or close trails due

HIKING GEAR ESSENTIALS CHECKLIST

Use this list as a starting point for your own personal hiking must-haves:
- First-aid kit and insect repellent
- Flashlight
- Food and water
- Rain jacket and hat
- Sunglasses
- Trail maps
- Warm hat, gloves, and long underwear in the cold seasons
- Proper footwear

to unsafe conditions, so make sure you use a current map. Maps are available at every state park office and website, and most other county and regional parks offer their maps online.

TRAIL DUCKS AND BLAZES
The trails in this book are, for the most part, well-defined paths, but you can't always rely on what looks like the right way. Leaves and snow can obscure trails, well-trod offshoots can lead you astray, and after-dark conditions can make paths hard to see. Some trails use trails ducks or tree blazes to mark the way. These white or blue rectangular markings are painted at eye level on trees. By standing next to a tree blaze, you can look ahead to the next and thus find your way.

COMPASS AND GPS SYSTEMS
A compass puts a map into helpful perspective. Knowing which direction is north can help you periodically check in with your map to make sure you are where you think you are. It can be helpful to use your map and compass together a few times before you hit the trail.

Many hikers also use GPS devices or mobile apps to guide them while hiking. In addition to showing you your exact location, GPS can log the distance you've traveled, how long it has taken you, and other statistics.

First-Aid and Emergency Supplies
Having fun on the trail means staying safe. Having a small first-aid kit with you that includes basics like Band-Aids, a small flashlight, aspirin, and some sunscreen can come in extremely handy. A pocketknife, matches or a lighter, and a whistle can also help keep you safe if you need them.

BLISTER PREVENTION

Hikers can overcome bad weather, muddy trails, and wrong directions out on the trail, but it is hard to keep moving when you develop a nasty blister on your heel. Even the most trail-ready hikers can get blisters. It is best to prevent them from forming by keeping your feet dry, wearing boots or shoes that are broken-in and fit your feet along with good-fitting socks, and solidly planting your heel when taking a step.

If you feel a hot spot forming while you're out on the trail, stop and tend to it right away. Take off your boot and sock and apply a Band-Aid or moleskin to the irritated area. Change out socks that have holes in them, as well. If you don't have any treatment items with you, take a rest and let the pain subside. If you are close to the trailhead, consider returning to your vehicle to get first-aid materials.

ON THE TRAIL
Wildlife, Plants, and Insects

There's a reason people joke that the mosquito is Minnesota's state bird. There are millions of them. Hikers will encounter insects, wildlife, and flora on all of these trails every season of the year (even winter!). Knowing what you might run into can help you prepare.

BEARS

Minnesota is home to one of the most densely populated areas of black bears in the country. While most of the animals you'll see in the Twin Cities are not bears, much of the habitat in the surrounding area is home to them. Bear encounters are rare, but you should know what to do in case you have a run-in.

Here are some tips for avoiding bears:
- Avoid carrying odorous foods.
- Make noise. Bears hate to be surprised, so let them know you are coming by singing, whistling, or talking with your hiking partner(s).
- Travel with someone else or in a group.
- Bears are most active during dawn and dusk. Plan your hikes during the day and stay on marked trails.

If you do encounter a bear on your hike:
- Remain calm and avoid sudden movements.
- Do not approach the bear. Give it plenty of space.
- Let the bear know that you are human. Talk to it and wave your arms. Bears have bad eyesight, and if one is unable to identify you, it may come closer for a better look.
- Never run from a bear. Running can elicit a chase.
- If the bear approaches you, distract it by throwing something on the ground near it. If this deters the bear's attention, walk away while it is distracted.

LOCAL NATIVE AMERICAN HISTORY AND CULTURE

Minnesota has a rich Native American history and culture. In Mille Lacs Kathio State Park, evidence of Native American villages dates back more than 9,000 years. Several of the trails in this book pass through or near lands that Native Americans consider sacred. Pike Island, Lake Ogechie, and Big Island (to name just a few) were the sites of early Native American settlements and gathering places. The Stone Arch Bridge, on the St. Anthony Falls Heritage Trail in downtown Minneapolis, marks a spot where tribes from all over the region gathered to trade and practice rituals. Several areas in the state have been recognized as national historical sites by the federal government. Learning about the area's Native American roots will enrich your hiking experience. The **Minnesota Historical Society** (www.mnhs.org) is a wonderful resource for Native American history and information.

- If you carry pepper spray, make sure you are trained in its use and can trust it if a bear attacks you.
- Never feed a bear.

BIRDS

One of North America's major bird migration corridors passes over Minnesota and the Twin Cities area, making it a bird-watcher's paradise. Walking the trails in this book during the spring and fall migration seasons is highly recommended. Not only will the beauty of the birds astound you, but you will get a deeper understanding of why nature conservation efforts in this state are so important. Thousands of birds and animal species are dependent on Minnesota's critical habitat areas for food, nesting, and shelter. Without places like the lush Minnesota River Valley, the dense forests north of the metro area, and the numerous freshwater lakes and rivers that blanket our landscape, these animals would quickly become endangered.

RARE WILDLIFE

The timber rattler, Blanding's turtle, and green heron are just a few of the rare species of wildlife that call Minnesota their home. The combination of wetlands, lakes, forests, and rivers make this area of the Upper Midwest a haven for creatures like the pine marten, long-legged fisher, common tern, and many others.

FLORA

The area surrounding the Twin Cities is home to a wide variety of habitats and a diverse selection of flowers, grasses, trees, and shrubs. Having knowledge of the plants that surround you can make your hike more enjoyable and more comfortable.

Wildflowers abound in the plush forests and grasslands that surround the Twin

LEAVE NO TRACE

Follow the Leave No Trace guidelines to keep natural spaces beautiful and enjoyable. These are the basic rules:

- Preserve the past: Examine, but do not touch, cultural or historic structures and artifacts.
- Leave rocks, plants, and other natural objects as you find them.
- Avoid introducing or transporting nonnative species.
- Do not build structures or furniture, or dig trenches.
- Pack it in, pack it out. Inspect your campsite and rest areas for trash or spilled food. Pack out all trash and leftover food.
- Observe wildlife from a distance. Do not follow or approach animals.
- Never feed animals. Feeding wildlife damages their health, alters natural behaviors, and exposes them to predators and other dangers.
- Control pets at all times, or leave them at home.

Cities. Indian paintbrush, butterfly weed, blooming milkweed, wild daisies, purple coneflowers, wild asters, and lupines grow thick in the grasslands, covering the rolling hills with color. Wetland plants, including wild irises, pitcher plants, and orchids take root in the wet soil. Growing among the trees, spring ephemerals like the rare dwarf trout lily, bloodroot, and snow trillium poke their blossoming heads into the sun for a few weeks.

Most of the flora in Minnesota is harmless, but some plants, like poison ivy, should be avoided. Remember the saying, "Leaves of three, let it be," which is a good way of identifying and avoiding this itchy weed that grows in small patches low to the ground. Other plants to avoid include purple fireweed and stinging nettle, which cause painful itching, skin irritation, and rashes. Wearing long pants and keeping your ankles covered can prevent unpleasant encounters.

INSECTS AND TICKS

Late spring through mid-autumn is insect season in Minnesota (although some varieties can be found thriving throughout the winter!). Mosquitoes, wood and deer ticks, horseflies, gnats, wasps, and other biting/stinging insects are unavoidable. The best way to protect yourself is to cover your skin and wear a hat.

Minnesota is home to 13 different types of ticks, including the black-legged tick, which can carry Lyme disease. If you notice a tick on you, remove it immediately, identify it when you get home, and watch for symptoms. Most Lyme disease symptoms occur one to three weeks after a tick bite and can include flu-like symptoms such as nausea, headaches, muscle soreness, fever, neck stiffness, and rashes. See a doctor immediately if you suspect that you have Lyme disease.

Trail Etiquette

HIKING WITH DOGS

If you hike with your dog, remember to follow appropriate trail etiquette. Please keep your dog on a leash and have a waste disposal plan to keep trails safe and clean. Check ahead of time to make sure the trail you are hiking allows dogs.

PROTECTING THE OUTDOORS

We enjoy the outdoors largely for its natural beauty. You can help keep it enjoyable for everyone by following Leave No Trace rules and by not marking trees, rocks, or other natural landmarks with knives, pens, or paint. Treat trails and parks with respect so everyone can enjoy them.

TWIN CITIES METRO AREA

The Minneapolis and St. Paul metro area is a hidden treasure for hikers, with the two cities boasting more than 300 parks and open spaces. The hiking and walking trails that are woven throughout the cities create a system with a combined length that totals more than 200 miles, touring recreational lakes, the epic Mississippi River, babbling Minnehaha Creek, and a world-renowned public rose garden. Amazingly, every mile is contained within the city limits. These hikes lead through vast floodplain forests, switchback up limestone bluffs, and meander past waterfalls and historic neighborhoods. These trails give new meaning to urban adventuring. Take time to explore the vast parklands that make Minneapolis and St. Paul two of the most hikable cities in the country, and you will see city life in an entirely different light.

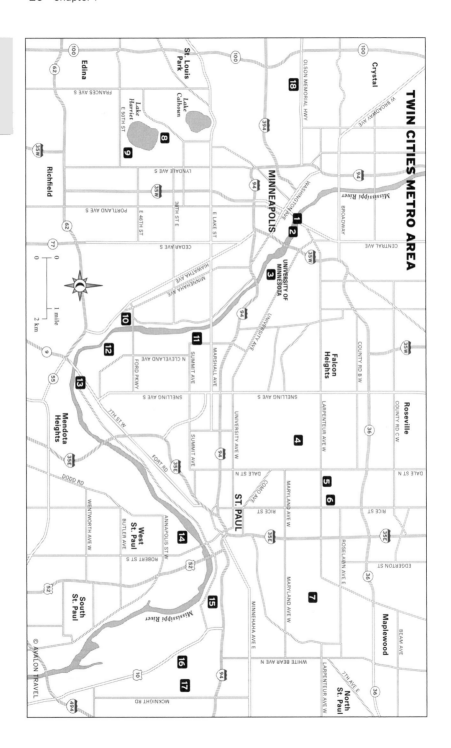

TRAIL NAME	LEVEL	DISTANCE	TIME	ELEVATION	PAGE
1 Nicollet and Boom Islands	Easy	1.6 mi	1 hr	Negligible	22
2 St. Anthony Falls Heritage Trail and Pillsbury Islands	Easy	2.25 mi	1.5 hr	100 ft	25
3 East River Flats to Old Wagon Road Trail	Easy	3.75 mi	2 hr	50 ft	27
4 Como Lake	Easy	1.67 mi	45 min	Negligible	30
5 Reservoir Woods Trail	Easy	1.5 mi	45 min	Negligible	33
6 Trout Brook Regional Trail	Easy	2 mi	1 hr	Negligible	36
7 Lake Phalen	Easy	3.2 mi	1.5 hr	Negligible	38
8 Lake Harriet	Easy	2.75 mi	1.25 hr	Negligible	41
9 Minnehaha Creek from Lake Harriet to Minnehaha Falls	Moderate	10 mi	5 hr	Negligible	44
10 Minnehaha Falls	Easy	2 mi	1 hr	50 ft	47
11 Two Bridges Loop	Moderate/strenuous	7.1 mi	3.5-4 hr	200 ft	50
12 Hidden Falls Shoreline Trail	Easy	3.75 mi	2 hr	40 ft	53
13 Crosby Farm Loop	Easy/moderate	4.2 mi	2.25 hr	50 ft	56
14 Harriet Island to Cherokee Bluffs	Moderate/strenuous	4.25 mi	2.5-3 hr	200 ft	59
15 Indian Mounds Loop	Easy	1.75 mi	1 hr	75 ft	62
16 Point Douglas Trail	Easy	3.5 mi	2 hr	Negligible	65
17 Battle Creek Loop	Easy	1.5 mi	1 hr	80 ft	67
18 Theodore Wirth Wildflower Trail	Easy	2.8 mi rt	1.5-2 hr	Negligible	69

1 NICOLLET AND BOOM ISLANDS
Nicollet Island Park, Minneapolis

Distance: 1.6 miles round-trip

Duration: 1 hour

Elevation Change: Negligible

Effort: Easy

Trail: Paved, packed turf

Users: Hikers, wheelchair users, leashed dogs

Season: Year-round

Passes/Fees: None

Maps: Park maps available at www.minneapolisparks.org/about_us/maps

Contact: Minneapolis Park & Recreation Board, 612/230-6400, www.minneapolisparks.org, 6am-10pm daily

View the Minneapolis skyline from the top of St. Anthony Falls.

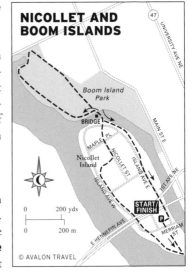

These two islands provide excellent urban hiking trails and a great view of the Minneapolis skyline. Both of the islands are just north of downtown Minneapolis in the Mississippi River. The trail provides a view of historic river-town neighborhoods upstream of St. Anthony Falls.

Start the Hike
Walk from the parking lot straight through the park to the southern end of the island. From the promenade on the lower end of the island, you can view the **1858 horseshoe dam** just above St. Anthony Falls—the first ever built on the Mississippi. Take a right and follow the paved trail along the island's western end.

This section of the park features the historic **Nicollet Island Pavilion,** built in 1893 as the William Bros. Boiler Works. The upper end of the island is a 19th-century residential district of 43 homes with architectural styles dating from the

The southern shore of Nicollet Island lies just above St. Anthony Falls.

1860s to the 1890s, when Minneapolis was a rapidly growing mill-city boomtown. The path follows **Island Avenue** and gives a spectacular view of the river and downtown Minneapolis. The fringes of the island are lined with some oak and maple trees, though most of the land is developed.

One-fifth of a mile from the parking lot, a paved walking trail leads through the park at the upper end of the island. Follow the trail to **Nicollet Street** and take a left. You will cross **Maple Place** and continue on the trail until you reach the water. Take a left here and cross the old railroad bridge, which has been converted into a walking path bridge. This bridge connects Nicollet Island to Boom Island.

Boom Island is a spacious park with a leisurely atmosphere. With 25 acres of open grassy areas, a large prairie restoration meadow with wild roses and daisies, a picnic area and shelter, boat launch, and riverside promenade, it is an urban paradise. While the skyscrapers of Minneapolis jut into the sky just a mile away, this breezy, open field is a wonderful respite from city life. A channel once separated Boom Island from the riverbank, but over time the area was filled. Prairie restoration efforts are now the focus of the space.

After crossing the **old railroad bridge,** follow the trail to your left. This takes you near the water and along the riverside promenade. The paved path loops around Boom Island and returns you to the bridge. As you approach the bridge, the last 0.25 mile borders a large meadow of wildflowers and prairie grasses. Take a moment to look at the many butterflies, birds, and bumblebees that give color and music to this beautiful area.

Hop back onto Nicollet Island and follow the gravel trail along the shore below Island Avenue that leads to a set of railroad tracks. The trail merges with Island Avenue here and heads back to Nicollet Island Park and the parking lot.

Shorten the Hike

From Nicollet Island Park, you can take a left and cross the Hennepin Avenue Bridge toward downtown and take a right onto West River Parkway for 0.75 mile. Cross the river again on the Plymouth Avenue Bridge and take a right into Boom Island Park for more views of the river and to turn this hike into a 1.5-mile loop.

Directions

From Minneapolis, head north across the Hennepin Avenue Bridge and exit right into the Nicollet Island parking lot.

Public Transportation: Bus route 61 stops at Hennepin Avenue and Wilder Street.

☑ ST. ANTHONY FALLS HERITAGE TRAIL AND PILLSBURY ISLANDS

Stone Arch Bridge and Mill Ruins Park, Minneapolis

Best: Historical Hikes, Waterfalls

Distance: 2.25 miles round-trip

Duration: 1.5 hours

Elevation Change: 100 feet

Effort: Easy

Trail: Paved, packed turf, brick

Users: Hikers, leashed dogs

Season: Year-round

Passes/Fees: None

Maps: Park maps available at www.minneapolisparks.org/about_us/maps

Contact: Minneapolis Park & Recreation Board, 100 Portland Ave., 612/230-6400, www.minneapolisparks.org, 6am-midnight daily

---

View the largest waterfall on the Mississippi, explore the islands under the Pillsbury factory, and see historic Main Street Park.

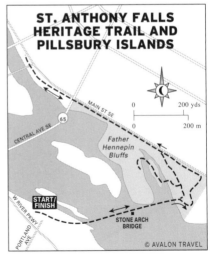

ST. ANTHONY FALLS HERITAGE TRAIL AND PILLSBURY ISLANDS

© AVALON TRAVEL

Once a railroad bridge built by the world's wealthiest railroad tycoon, the Stone Arch Bridge is now a pedestrian path that connects historic downtown to modern-day downtown Minneapolis. This trail provides glimpses into centuries of history and gives a bird's-eye view of St. Anthony Falls.

Start the Hike

From the parking lot at Mills Ruins Park, walk along the bench-lined paved path up to the entrance to the **Stone Arch Bridge.** It is a Historic Civil Engineering Landmark, added to the National Register of Historic Places in 1971 as part of the St. Anthony Falls Historic District. The bridge is just short of being 0.5 mile long and will give you the city's best view of St. Anthony Falls. The cataract at your left is the largest on the entire 2,200-mile Mississippi River. When you **cross the bridge,** keep to your right.

A railing and an informative plaque give a bit of history about the area, and a small wildflower garden is planted at the site. The garden blooms with Indian paintbrush and blazing stars, memorializing the place where it is believed that Father Hennepin first viewed the Falls of St. Anthony in 1680. Just beyond the garden, a sidewalk path curves west through the open picnic and amphitheater area atop **Father Hennepin Bluffs.** Follow the path through the oak and maple trees to the walkway that leads along historic Main Street in **Main Street Park.** Lined with restaurants, the historic Pillsbury factory, and architecture from Minneapolis's boomtown days, historic Main Street leads to the **Hennepin Avenue Bridge.** Turn around here and cross the street if you wish to take in the other side of the thoroughfare. This river path and the Stone Arch Bridge are part of the longer St. Anthony Falls Heritage Trail, which loops through downtown.

When you return to the bluffs, veer to the right on the sidewalk path that leads to the yellow bandstand. Keep walking toward the river on your right and look for the set of wooden steps that lead down to the islands of **Pillsbury Park.** The steps are steep, so make sure to use the handrail. At the bottom, take a right and follow the rocky trail bridged with wooden steps and footbridges through a small set of islands at the foot of the falls and under the historic Pillsbury factory. You will more than likely see grebes and great blue herons wading in the backwater of the falls amid the islands.

Take the stairs back up to the bluffs. The **bridge entrance** is about 100 feet ahead of you on your right. Walk back to the parking lot while taking another look at St. Anthony Falls. Just beyond the falls lie Nicollet Island and the Hennepin Avenue Bridge. Ahead of you on the return trip, you will be able to see the world-famous Guthrie Theater, the Mill City Museum, and the ruins of Mill Ruins Park to your left.

Extend the Hike
At the end of the bridge on the return trip, take a left on West River Parkway to see the ruins of Mill Ruins Park and the Mill City Museum along a planked boardwalk. This venture will add 0.25 mile to your hike.

Directions
From Minneapolis, take West River Parkway to Mill Ruins Park at the intersection of Portland Avenue. Parking is under the bridge in the park.

Public Transportation: Bus route 22H stops at 5th Avenue and Washington Avenue.

3 EAST RIVER FLATS TO OLD WAGON ROAD TRAIL

East River Flats Park, Minneapolis

Distance: 3.75 miles round-trip

Duration: 2 hours

Elevation Change: 50 feet

Effort: Easy

Trail: Paved, packed turf

Users: Hikers, cyclists, inline skaters, leashed dogs

Season: Year-round

Passes/Fees: None

Maps: Park maps available at www.minneapolisparks.org/about_us/maps

Contact: Minneapolis Park & Recreation Board, 351 East River Pkwy., 612/230-6400, www.minneapolisparks.org, 6am-midnight daily

---

Enjoy a beautiful bluff walk on the Mississippi, from East River Flats to the old Meeker Island Lock and Dam.

East River Flats Park is one of the easiest access points to the Mississippi River Gorge and waterfront on the east side of the river. The limestone bluffs here rise only 25 feet, which made it a choice spot for a paved walking path. The park is a 26-acre stretch of land that lies upon the flat deposits formed by the inner side of a large bend in the river. Just below the University of Minnesota's Minneapolis campus, this open, grassy park has a sandy beach and a recreation field that is almost always in use.

Start the Hike

Start this hike by following the 0.5-mile loop around the flats from the parking lot. A **paved walkway** takes you along the river's shore and right to the foot of

The Old Wagon Road Trail near Meeker Island is a national historical site.

the bluffs. Some remnants of floodplain forest, mostly manifested by oak trees, are still present on the flats and the bluff face.

Once you return to the parking lot, walk away from the river onto **Mississippi River Boulevard.** Take a right onto the paved path that leads southeast. This trail follows the top of the bluff along the eastern edge of the **Mississippi River Gorge.** This is a well-maintained area that has benches, drinking fountains, informational plaques, and kiosks interspersed throughout the park pathway.

From **East River Flats Park,** walk away from the river, following the path to the right as it leaves the park. To get to the **Old Wagon Road Trail,** you will walk for 1.25 miles along East River Parkway. Due to its close proximity to the University of Minnesota, this portion of the hike is a shared trail area. Bicyclists and inline skaters frequent the path in summer, and many people walk their dogs or sunbathe in the area.

Approximately 0.5 mile from the flats, you will cross the **Franklin Avenue bridge.** Continue along the trail, taking time to look at the opposite shore from your height on the bluffs. Several unmarked trails lead down to the riverside along this portion of the hike. You can take some time to explore these offshoot trails and enjoy the shade of the trees that grow on the steep slopes leading to the water. Large oak and maple trees line the bluff sides and create cool, shady areas on either side of the river. Squirrels and rabbits abound here, and occasionally you may see a raccoon or a shy fox. Deer are rare in the city but can sometimes be seen at dawn or dusk feeding along the tree line.

Shortly after passing under a large railroad bridge, you will come to the **Old Wagon Road Trail** on your right at the site of the former **Meeker Island Lock and Dam.** Meeker Island was the location of the first lock and dam facility on the Upper Mississippi River, built in 1912. A decade later, a hydroelectric dam was built downstream, which negated the need for the Meeker Island facility. The dam was demolished, although some ruins of the lock remain. Tops of the old lock walls are sometimes visible during low water periods. The Meeker Island Lock and Dam ruins were added to the National Register of Historic Places in 2003, and a St. Paul Parks & Recreation project developed the Old Wagon Road Trail that leads to the site. The switchback trail is just short of 0.25 mile long and leads to a shady **riverfront viewing area** across from the old lock.

When you are ready to head back, climb up the switchback and retrace your steps to the flats. The return trip will treat you to views of the Minneapolis skyline and the artful architecture of the University of Minnesota campus.

Extend the Hike

At the top of the Old Wagon Road Trail, continue southeast along the river bluff for 0.75 mile to see the Shadow Falls viewing area at the end of Summit Avenue. This extra stretch will add 1.25 miles to your hike. Shadow Falls is a 40-foot trickling waterfall in a ravine that leads to the river.

Directions

From St. Paul, head west on I-94 for 6.2 miles. Exit onto Huron Boulevard and take a left on Fulton Street East for three blocks. Turn right onto East River Parkway just past the University of Minnesota Cancer Center. Turn left into the East River Flats parking lot.

Public Transportation: Bus route 144 stops at the Huron Station.

4 COMO LAKE
Como Park, St. Paul

Distance: 1.67 miles round-trip

Duration: 45 minutes

Elevation Change: Negligible

Effort: Easy

Trail: Paved

Users: Hikers, cyclists, wheelchair users, leashed dogs

Season: Year-round

Passes/Fees: None

Maps: Maps available at www.stpaul.gov

Contact: St. Paul Parks & Recreation, 1199 Midway Pkwy., 651/266-6400, www. stpaul.gov, sunrise-11pm daily

---

This easy walk rambles through the shady oaks, native tallgrass, and open fields surrounding Como Lake.

The land around Como Lake was set aside in 1891 to preserve open wilderness areas for city-dwelling St. Paulites. One of the metro area's most popular parks, Como Park includes the lake, a theme park, the Como Zoo, the Como Conservatory, and the Japanese Garden with goldfish ponds. Full of open fields, majestic oak trees, and "Oz"-like buildings, the park hearkens back to the early boomtown days of St. Paul and is a favorite for students looking for a quiet study spot and for people unwinding after work.

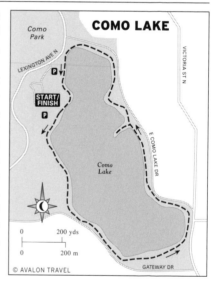

Start the Hike

Begin at the parking lot of the architecturally striking **Grand Como Pavilion,** which is situated on the western side of the lake, and head counterclockwise around the water. The wide paved path is shared with bicyclists, so make sure to stay on the designated walking area. The walkway curves around the southern bend of the lake for the first 0.25 mile. A portion of the southern shore is part of St. Paul's natural habitat restoration program. In the summer months, you will find yourself amid lakeshore grasses and bright prairie flowers like asters, milkweed, and wild daisies waving in the breeze.

As the trail arcs over to the east side of the lake, it winds beneath gnarled oak trees, which provide a decent amount of refreshing shade. This stretch is a popular spot for anglers. At the 0.75-mile mark, there is a **memorial bench** that looks across the

These gnarly pine trees provide shade on the southern end of Como Lake.

water at the pavilion and beyond to the wide-open grassy fields that stretch out from the lake. With the shore restoration project and the pine grove of the southern shore to your left and the sweep of the blue lake at your feet, this is one of the best panoramas of the park. A half mile farther up the trail, a small peninsula called **Duck Point** juts out into the lake, just wide enough for the path. If an angler isn't stationed there with fishing pole in hand, this little nook makes a great resting spot amid the soft lapping of the waves. A trip along this same stretch in autumn treats hikers to rich fall colors, from the browns of the oak leaves to the golden yellows of the maple leaves that are scattered throughout the western fields of the park.

The northern bend of the lake is closer to the more populated areas of the park and the traffic of **Lexington Parkway.** Zoo and conservatory visitors, dog walkers, and brown-bag lunchers frequent this stretch of the trail. Here, near the golf course, the path oxbows through manicured lawns and brightly colored flower beds maintained by the park service in the spring and summer. As the arc of the walkway straightens out toward the south, it branches out in several directions leading toward the **zoo, conservatory, and picnic area.** Keep to the left and finish the final 0.25 mile to end up back at the pavilion.

Make It a Day Trip

Visit the impressive **Como Conservatory, Japanese Garden,** or **Como Zoo** just 0.5 mile away to turn this hike into an entire afternoon or day trip. After circling the lake, take a right at the stone waterfall and follow the sidewalk path through the oak trees toward the conservatory. Signs will direct you to the Japanese Garden. Look for the huge goldfish the park keeps in the garden pond.

Directions

From St. Paul, head west on I-94 for 3.5 miles, exit onto Lexington Parkway, and drive north for approximately 1.5 miles (30 blocks). Turn right on Nusbaumer Drive into the Grand Como Pavilion parking lot.

Public Transportation: Bus route 3 has a stop at Como Avenue and Lexington Parkway. A METRO Green Line light rail station is at Lexington Avenue and University Avenue.

5 RESERVOIR WOODS TRAIL

Reservoir Woods, Roseville

Distance: 2.9 miles round-trip

Duration: 1.75 hours

Elevation Change: 60 feet

Effort: Easy

Trail: Paved, gravel, packed turf

Users: Hikers, wheelchair users, dogs

Season: Year-round

Passes/Fees: None

Maps: Maps available on the park website

Contact: City of Roseville Parks & Recreation, 1901 Alta Vista Dr., 651/792-7006, www.cityofroseville.com, sunrise-sunset

This large park, heavily wooded with groves of red pine trees, is preserved as a natural area and open space.

If you want to get buried in the woods without leaving the city, take a hike through Reservoir Woods. The 52-acre park is right on the St. Paul city limits, and is reserved as a Ramsey County Open Space site. The area houses a 30-million-gallon underground reservoir that was operated by the city of St. Paul until 1997.

Start the Hike

With **Larpenteur Avenue** to your back, take the trail on the right side of the parking lot near the **map kiosk.** The paved trail goes downhill into a wetland area past the **fenced dog park.** At the bottom of the hill, the trail enters a pine grove and takes on the feel of a large, remote outdoors area. The thick forest and lower elevation of the park make it a quiet and peaceful place removed from most of the sounds of traffic.

Orange mileage markers are positioned every tenth of a mile along the paved walkway. Stands of red (Norway) pine are periodically marked with signs that explain their scientific name and their role in the native habitat.

At the **0.3-mile marker,** a sheltered bench offers shaded seating, and an information area features a large map that shows the trail you are on in relation to the surrounding area.

These majestic pine trees sway in the breeze along the Reservoir Woods Trail.

Take a left at the rest area and follow the trail through a lighted tunnel under the **Dale Street road bridge.** The trail winds through the quiet forest for another 0.5 mile. Look for the whitetail deer that love this secluded forest oasis. You may also see skunks, rabbits, and raccoons. At the **0.8-mile marker,** a planked walkway leads to a small overlook with railings and benches. Enjoy the view of a thick stand of red pine and a seasonal stream.

This heavily wooded city park is an urban refuge for raccoons, groundhogs, nesting songbirds, and swans. When the city of Roseville created Reservoir Woods Park, the land was intentionally left in a very forest-like state. Little development has been done other than building a paved trail through the park and maintaining various natural-surface trails.

At the **1-mile marker,** the trail curves right and up a ridge to a more open area near another grove of pine trees. A portable restroom is usually available here. One-fifth mile later, just past a **signal tower,** the trail opens up to a meadowland of grasses and flowers. Violets, clover, and some Indian paintbrush can be seen here.

The pavement ends at the **1.4-mile marker** at Victoria Street near the Roselawn Cemetery. Take a left and walk through the red gate onto a gravel path. The gravel leads to the right and will take you through the meadowland you saw just 0.2 mile back on the paved trail. Walk through the meadow and follow the **dirt trail** until it loops back to the paved trail. Follow the path back through the woods to your starting point.

Extend the Hike

The park's paved trail connects to the McCarrons Lake path and Trout Brook Regional trails to the east, side paths along Roselawn Avenue and Lexington Avenue to the west, a side path along Dale Street to the north, and the parking area off of Lexington to the south. These options can add anywhere from 0.5 to 2 miles to your hike.

Directions

From St. Paul, head north on Rice Street for 3 miles. Take a left on Larpenteur Avenue for 0.7 mile and take a right into the Reservoir Woods parking lot across from Mackubin Street; it's marked with a large wooden sign and map kiosk.

Public Transportation: Bus route 65 stops at Dale Street and Larpenteur Avenue.

6 TROUT BROOK REGIONAL TRAIL

Lake McCarrons County Park, St. Paul

Distance: 2 miles round-trip

Duration: 1 hour

Elevation Change: Negligible

Effort: Easy

Trail: Paved

Users: Hikers, cyclists, wheelchair users, leashed dogs

Season: Year-round

Passes/Fees: None

Maps: Maps available on the park website

Contact: Lake McCarrons County Park, 1765 North Rice Street, 651/748-2500, www.ramseycounty.us, 9am-9pm daily

---

The Trout Brook Trail leads through undeveloped wetlands surrounding in St. Paul's Eastside.

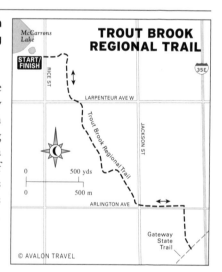

This hike is geared more toward the urban adventurer. Known mostly by bikers taking a divergent route from the popular Gateway State biking trail, Trout Brook Regional Trail is a nicely paved path that follows a set of railroad tracks, skirts a city pond, slips past housing developments, and cuts through an industrial district on St. Paul's North End.

Start the Hike

From **Lake McCarrons County Park,** take a right on **Rice Street** to the crosswalk. Pick up the trail on the other side of the road and follow it across a set of **railroad tracks.** The trail makes a sharp right-hand turn here and runs between the brook on the left and the railroad tracks on the right.

For the next 0.25 mile, you will walk along the brook and through the open grass and wetland areas that surround the waterway. Wild daisies, violets, and clover poke through the grass until the path reaches **Larpenteur Avenue.** Cross the street at the crosswalk into the trees and resume along the paved path.

Over the next 0.5 mile, you walk through a shady wooded area of maple trees, following the reedy shores of the brook. You will walk under the **Wheelock Parkway bridge,** and shortly thereafter (approximately 0.25 mile after crossing Larpenteur Avenue) the brook widens after passing through a **culvert bridge.** The trail skirts around small ponds here in a low, wetland area that slows the brook. Ducks, geese, and the occasional swan frequent this area. You may also see red-winged blackbirds, raccoons, and wood ducks. Although deer aren't frequently seen in the city, you have a much greater chance of seeing one here than almost anywhere else. Look to the tree line and watch for their tracks along the trail.

On the far side of the largest of these ponds, the trail crosses to the opposite side of the brook. You walk along the edge of a residential area on the edge of a vast wetland area full of cattails and reeds. This low field is full of chirping frogs, flitting birds, and brightly colored, buzzing dragonflies. You will almost certainly see deer tracks along the edge of this wet area, especially near that large pond.

The paved path eventually emerges from the cattails and deposits you on **Jackson Street.** The last 0.25-mile stretch to the turnaround point is through a more urbanized area. Take a right on Jackson Street to the intersection of **Arlington Avenue.** Cross the street and take a left on Arlington. In 500 feet, turn right on **L'Orient Street** for another 400 feet until the trail meets the paved **Gateway State biking trail.**

Follow the path back to Lake McCarrons County Park, this time headed upstream along the brook. Keep your eyes open for deer and other wildlife that may be grazing around the cattail and pond area.

Extend the Hike
Take a right on the Gateway State Trail at the end of L'Orient Street to walk past the large pond and walking bridge to Cayuga Park; this adds an extra 0.5 mile to your hike. The trail is more exposed than the Trout Brook walkway, but if you don't mind the city walk, give it a try.

Directions
From St. Paul, head north on Rice Street for 3 miles. Turn left into the Lake McCarrons Beach park entrance and parking lot.

Public Transportation: Bus route 62 stops at Rice Street and Roselawn Avenue.

7 LAKE PHALEN

Phalen Regional Park, St. Paul

Distance: 3.2 miles round-trip

Duration: 1.5 hours

Elevation Change: Negligible

Effort: Easy

Trail: Paved

Users: Hikers, wheelchair users, leashed dogs

Season: Year-round

Passes/Fees: None

Maps: Maps available on the park website

Contact: St. Paul Parks & Recreation, 1600 Phalen Dr., 651/266-6400, www.stpaul.gov, 7:30am-4:30pm Mon.-Fri.

Serene Lake Phalen features oak savannas, shoreline restoration, and a sense of openness in picturesque Phalen Regional Park.

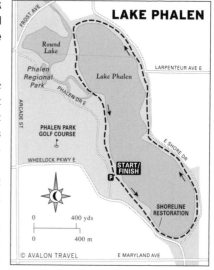

Lake Phalen is the most mysterious lake in the Twin Cities. The small delta at the mouth of Phalen Creek is thought to be the place at which Father Louis Hennepin landed on his journey to discover the falls of St. Anthony in 1680. The creek that once flowed southwest through Swede Hollow was entombed underground at the turn of the 20th century by railroad companies. The creek is now contained in a cavernous 22-foot-high drainage tunnel, and the low delta that once spread into the Mississippi was filled in and used as a rail yard.

Phalen Regional Park has a popular golf course, a beach house, shore restoration areas, picnic and outdoor amphitheater areas, a fishing pier, a playground, and a tennis court. Mallards, swans, and grebes can be seen among the reeds near the shoreline.

the southeastern shore of Lake Phalen

Start the Hike

From the beach house parking lot, walk down to the water and take a right at the **beach.** The southwestern side of the lake is lined with rustic wooden fencing protecting shore restoration areas along the lake. Willow trees hug the water, and the grassy open areas narrow as the trail soon merges with **Wheelock Parkway.** Wrap around the southern edge of the lake and follow the trail north along **East Shore Drive.** When you cross the large **stone culvert bridge,** you can see the beach house and grassy fields full of thick oak trees, clover flowers, and wild daisies at the trailhead.

The creek once cut a large ravine through the area and is rumored to have been lined with several caves. Some say that Lake Phalen itself is rife with underwater caves. Whether it is or not, Phalen is easily one of the deepest lakes in the area, which adds to its mystery.

For the next mile, the trail hugs East Shore Drive between the lake and the road. At the north end of the lake, the trail enters the more open park grounds. As you curve toward the south, you will walk between Lake Phalen to your left and the smaller **Round Lake** to your right. Stay on the walkway closest to Lake Phalen and you will cross **Keller Creek,** which connects the two bodies of water. Just on the other side of the bridge is the fishing pier. **Lake Phalen** is one of the most heavily fished metro area lakes.

The last 0.5 mile of the hike takes you through the picnic pavilion and playground and past the **Lakeside Activities Center.** From there, the beach house parking lot is just 0.25 mile ahead.

Extend the Hike

At the northern end of the lake, veer right at the parking lot and take the walkway around adjoining Round Lake to take in more of the aquatic plants and waterfowl of the park. The diversion will add 0.5 mile to your hike.

Directions

From St. Paul, head north on I-35 East. Exit right on Larpenteur Avenue East. Turn right at Arcade, then left onto Wheelock Parkway, and then left onto Phalen Drive East. Park in the beach house parking lot on your right.

Public Transportation: Bus route 64 stops at Wheelock Parkway and Maryland Avenue.

8 LAKE HARRIET
Lake Harriet, Minneapolis

Distance: 2.75 miles round-trip

Duration: 1.25 hours

Elevation Change: Negligible

Effort: Easy

Trail: Paved

Users: Hikers, wheelchair users, leashed dogs

Season: Year-round

Passes/Fees: Parking $0.50 per hour

Maps: Maps available at www.minneapolisparks.org/about_us/maps/

Contact: Minneapolis Park & Recreation Board, 4135 West Lake Harriet Pkwy., 612/230-6400, www.minneapolisparks.org, dawn-dusk daily

Lake Harriet is a beautiful urban lake with swimming beaches, hiking trails, a bandstand, and serene shoreline.

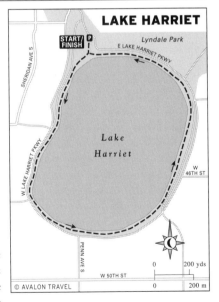

A staple of the Chain of Lakes system, Lake Harriet is bordered by Lyndale Park and its rose garden and features a park-like path along its entire shoreline. A trail at the northwest end leads to Lake Calhoun, and another at the southeast corner connects the trail system to Minnehaha Creek.

Start the Hike
From the parking lot, walk toward the **band shell.** The walking path starts between the lake and band shell. Move **counterclockwise** around the lake with the water to your left. On the lake side of the band shell is a **marina** where canoes and sailboats can be rented or stored for use. A nearby dock allows canoeists to access the water. Sailboats are on the lake virtually every day during the summer.

© JAKE KULJU

The beautiful bandshell on Lake Harriet can be seen from all points along the trail that circles the lake.

Continue walking along the western shore of the lake, making sure you are utilizing the **walking path** and not the biking path. Lake Harriet is part of the Grand Rounds bike trail system, which runs through the Twin Cities and is used by thousands of cyclists each year. A mile into the hike, you reach the southern edge of the lake directly across from the band shell. For the rest of the loop around the lake, the striking band shell is visible.

A mile farther up the trail, you near **Lyndale Park** and the **Lyndale Park Rose Garden.** The garden is the second-oldest public rose garden in the nation. Constructed in 1908, the 1.5-acre garden was designed by the "father of rose gardens," Theodore Wirth. In 1946, it was designated an official All America Rose Selections (AARS) test rose garden. The majestic Heffelfinger Fountain is on display on the patio amid the roses.

Lyndale Park also has gently rolling hills that feature beautiful oak savannas. Take a minute to walk in the shade of the beautiful trees and rest on soft slopes overlooking the lake. The last 0.25 mile back to the band shell is a breeze. You walk past the popular **north beach** and get a full view of the entire lake from north to south.

Extend the Hike

After returning to the band shell, take a right on Lake Harriet Parkway and follow it through William Berry Park to add a view of glimmering Lake Calhoun and an additional 0.75 mile to your hike.

Directions

From Minneapolis, take I-35 West south for 1 mile to the 35th/36th Street exit. Turn right at 35th Street East and left on Nicollet Avenue. Turn right on 36th Street West for 1.3 miles. At East Calhoun Parkway, turn left. Take another left on William Berry Parkway and drive into the East Lake Harriet Parkway parking lot.

9 MINNEHAHA CREEK FROM LAKE HARRIET TO MINNEHAHA FALLS

Minnehaha Parkway, Minneapolis

Distance: 10 miles round-trip

Duration: 5 hours

Elevation Change: Negligible

Effort: Moderate

Trail: Paved

Users: Hikers, leashed dogs

Season: Year-round

Passes/Fees: None

Maps: Maps available online at www.minneapolisparks.org/about_us/maps

Contact: Minneapolis Park & Recreation Board, 4135 West Lake Harriet Pkwy., 612/230-6400, www.minneapolisparks.org, dawn-dusk daily

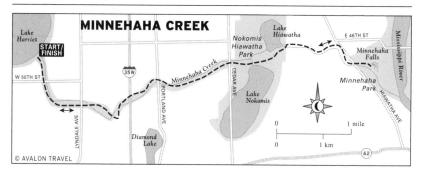

Walk along Minnehaha Creek to the famous 53-foot Minnehaha Falls near the Mississippi River.

Minnehaha Creek is a playful and picturesque tributary of the Mississippi River. The most popular section of the creek runs for 5 miles from Lake Harriet to Minnehaha Falls, culminating at the 53-foot waterfall at the center of Minnehaha Park. The falls are near the creek's confluence with the Mississippi River in a beautiful urban park.

Wooden footbridges like this one cross Minnehaha Creek intermittently on its way to the falls.

Start the Hike

From **Lake Harriet Parkway,** take a right at the intersection of **Minnehaha Parkway.** A paved path veers to the right of the parkway and leads along a small wooded waterway toward Minnehaha Creek itself. Like the Lake Harriet trail, the **Minnehaha Parkway trail** has a bike path and a walking path. Make sure you stay on the pedestrian-only trail. Violets grow in this shady area, and rabbits, squirrels, and sparrows all love the cover provided by these urban trees.

The trail meets the creek near 50th Street next to **Lynnhurst Field.** Follow the creek trail as it bends eastward. The creek's depth and speed vary depending on the time of year and the amount of recent rainfall. During long bouts of dryness in the summer, the creek can literally be reduced to a trickle, and the falls can nearly disappear. But during robust rains in the spring and summer, the creek quickly becomes a fast-moving and fairly deep channel that has surprising force.

About a mile from Lake Harriet, the trail dips under the **Lyndale Avenue bridge**—a particularly picturesque spot on the creek, with a wooden boardwalk that winds under the stone arch of the old bridge. There are some steps along the boardwalk that emerge on the other side of Lyndale Avenue, but nothing too serious. This hike has hardly any noticeable elevation change. Wheelchair users can use the paved bike path that crosses Lyndale Avenue above the creek. Half a mile from the Lyndale bridge, the trail passes under the I-35 West overpass and follows the creek northwest past **Portland Avenue.** As the creek nears Lake Nokomis, beautifully crafted bridges connect paths across the water at various points along the creek.

At **Bloomington Avenue,** stay on the walkway adjacent to Minnehaha Parkway. You are not immediately next to the creek here, but you will soon walk through **Lake Nokomis Park** and rejoin the creek near Lake Hiawatha as it flows from one lake to the other. Lake Nokomis may entice you to leave the trail to view the willow tree-lined lake and its beach. The trail and the creek cross Minnehaha Parkway on the northern side of Lake Nokomis and wind through a rolling oak savanna. A larger bridge takes you across the mouth of the creek at **Lake Hiawatha** and leads you to the crossing at 28th Avenue. Use the crosswalk here and descend the slope back to the creekside.

From here to the falls, the creek makes four large bends on its way downstream. Stay on the northern side of the creek during the next 0.5 mile and take a right at **Hiawatha Avenue** where the trail meets a T. This path brings you to the **Longfellow Gardens** adjacent to Minnehaha Park. Cross Minnehaha Avenue and continue to follow the creek to the falls viewing area.

You may want to rest here and enjoy the sights and sounds of the waterfall. Take the same path back to **Lake Harriet,** following the creek upstream this time.

Shorten the Hike
You can park a car at Minnehaha Park and shuttle back to your starting point to cut your hiking time in half. The falls is a lovely ending point, and this option still gives you a great 2-3-hour hike through this beautiful natural setting that runs through the city.

Directions
From Minneapolis, take I-35 West south for 2.2 miles to the 46th Street exit. Turn right on 46th Street East for 1 mile. Turn left at Humbolt Avenue South and right onto Minnehaha Parkway.

10 MINNEHAHA FALLS

Minnehaha Park, Minneapolis

Best: Waterfalls

Distance: 2 miles round-trip

Duration: 1 hour

Elevation Change: 50 feet

Effort: Easy

Trail: Paved, packed turf, gravel

Users: Hikers, leashed dogs

Season: Year-round

Passes/Fees: None

Maps: Maps available at www.minneapolisparks.org/about_us/maps/

Contact: Minneapolis Park & Recreation Board, 4801 South Minnehaha Dr., 612/230-6400, www.minneapolisparks.org, 6am-midnight daily

---

View the state's most famous waterfall in one of Minneapolis's oldest parks.

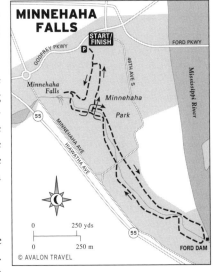

The scenery on this hike is some of the best in the city, including a dazzling waterfall, a babbling creek, native wildflowers, and the Mississippi River. The picnic grounds and recreation spaces are perennial neighborhood favorites. There is almost always music in the park on weekends, as well.

Start the Hike

Follow the **paved path** through the park gates near the drinking fountain. The trail heads 0.25 mile through an oak savanna **picnic area** toward the creek. In the summer, this portion of the park is usually full of people throwing Frisbees, walking their dogs, and barbecuing. As you near the creek, you walk past the bandstand and come to the stone wall

The famous Minnehaha Falls is a 53-foot cataract near the terminus of Minnehaha Creek. Just downstream the creek empties into the Mississippi River.

and railing that leads to the **viewing area** for the falls.

You will hear the falls before you see them. Minnehaha means "laughing waters," and you'll soon hear why. When they do come into sight, it is through silver birch trees that line the rim of the creek basin. The footprints of President Lyndon B. Johnson (preserved in cement) commemorate the spot he viewed the falls from on a visit to Minnesota.

Take the **stone stairway** to your left that leads below the falls, and soak in the spectacular view from a **footbridge** that crosses the creek just under the waterfall. When you are ready to move on, cross the bridge and follow the trail downstream as it runs adjacent to the creek. The trail leads through the small ravine cut by the creek and swings through an open grassy area. Turn left in a few hundred feet downstream from the falls and follow a **second stone bridge** over the creek. Turn right and keep following the trail, with the water to your right. After a bend in the creek, the path joins a wider **gravel walkway** that leads farther downstream. Stay on this path as it narrows into a packed **dirt trail.** This route takes you through the floodplain forest floor, through grassy creekside flower beds of wild daisies and creeping bellflowers to the rocky mouth of **Minnehaha Creek** as it becomes a tributary of the Mississippi River. This spot, just below **Ford Dam,** is a popular fishing hole for local anglers. All season long you are sure to find people in waders or casting from shore.

Cross the bridge at the river's mouth and head upstream on the opposite bank. You can see the shoreline and the trail on the other side of the creek that you previously traveled. Take your time to spot the native wildflowers and the diverse trees in this portion of the park, including oak, silver maple, basswood, birch, elm, and cottonwood.

When you return to the bend in the creek that led you to the gravel path, cross over the water on the **stone bridge** at the mouth of the small ravine. Walk 0.2 mile across the open grassy area and up a **gravel path** to the sidewalk. Follow this path to your left back to the parking lot.

Extend the Hike

Cross Minnehaha Park Drive on the western edge of the park to enter the Longfellow Gardens. The garden area is a land bridge that goes over Hiawatha Avenue. The formal garden features a sundial, flowers planted in paisley patterns, and a pergola. Prairie flowers and grasses line the creek and outer edges of the garden. This will add an extra 0.25 mile to your hike.

Directions

From Minneapolis, drive east on Washington Avenue. Turn right onto Hiawatha Avenue/Highway 55 for 3.5 miles. Turn left at 46th Street East and right again onto Minnehaha Avenue. After the traffic circle, take the third exit and drive west on Godfrey Parkway. Turn right into Minnehaha Park parking lot just before 46th Avenue South.

Public Transportation: Bus route 27 stops at 46th Street and Minnehaha Avenue. A METRO Blue Line light rail station is at 46th Street and Hiawatha Avenue.

11 TWO BRIDGES LOOP

Mississippi Parkway, St. Paul

Best: River Hikes, Waterfalls

Effort: Moderate/strenuous

Distance: 7.1 miles round-trip

Duration: 3.5-4 hours

Elevation Change: 200 feet

Trail: Paved, packed turf, gravel

Users: Hikers, leashed dogs

Season: Year-round; cross-country skiing in winter

Passes/Fees: None

Maps: Maps available at www.stpaul.gov

Contact: St. Paul Parks & Recreation, 651/266-6400, www.stpaul.gov or Minneapolis Park & Recreation, 612/230-6400, www.minneapolisparks.org, dawn-dusk daily

---

Follow the Mississippi River gorge as the trail clings to the edges of the bluffs and descends into the bottomlands along the river's shore.

As far as urban wilderness exploration goes, this is as good as it gets. More than 7 miles of Mississippi River gorge trail fishtails through the floodplain forest and low bluffs along one of the most scenic portions of the river between St. Paul and Minneapolis.

Start the Hike

Begin by walking behind the railing at the western edge of the parking area and taking a right. The path leads out to a **rock outcropping** that overlooks the river and the skyline of Minneapolis. Take in the scenery and keep moving to your right. A **packed dirt trail** follows a stone wall for about 100 feet and then veers to the left and through the shady oak trees that surround a small ravine cut by **Shadow Falls.** The path leads to the top of the falls where you can watch the small stream that feeds it tumble into the gorge. Turn right here and follow the path as it merges with the paved walking trail along **Mississippi River Boulevard** at Cretin Avenue. Take a left on this walking path as it follows the river.

The path winds along the edge of the bluffs for 0.5 mile, leading to a stairway at the base of the **Lake Street bridge.** Climb the stairs and walk over the river.

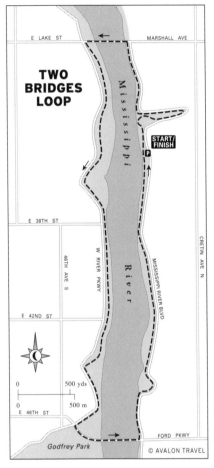

TWO BRIDGES LOOP

E LAKE ST   MARSHALL AVE

Mississippi

START/FINISH

E 38TH ST

CRETIN AVE N

46TH AVE S   W RIVER PKWY   MISSISSIPPI RIVER BLVD

River

E 42ND ST

0   500 yds
0   500 m
E 46TH ST

FORD PKWY

Godfrey Park   © AVALON TRAVEL

Upstream, to the north you will see the University of Minnesota's Minneapolis campus. To the south you will see the Ford Parkway bridge—the second bridge of the loop. Once you reach the Minneapolis side of the river, take a left and walk down to **West River Parkway.** Cross the street and take a right. In a few hundred feet, you will come to a set of stairs that leads down to the river. At the foot of the stairs, join up with the **packed dirt trail** that leads along the shoreline forest at the base of the low-rising bluffs. From here you will be able to see the rock formation at your starting point across the river.

Follow the trail as it moves through shady oaks, wild daisies, violets, and blooming milkweed flowers amid the river grasses that cover the area. Keep your eyes peeled for urban wildlife like rabbits, groundhogs, and raccoons that live near the river. About a third of the way to the **second bridge** (near 38th Street) the bluffs move closer to the riverbank, and the trail ascends along the **bluff walls** as they come flush with the water. This part of the hike can be challenging and will require some light climbing. Make sure your shoes have good ankle support, and you should hold on to trees for balance along the narrow parts of the trail on the edge of the bluff.

This river gorge area you are passing through is part of **Mississippi Park,** which merges with Godfrey Park and Minnehaha Park to the south. On both sides of the river, you will encounter great blue herons, whitetail deer, painted turtles, and possibly raccoons. Urban wildlife loves the lush, shady river gorge and often has small dens and nests among the rocks and trees.

Around **44th Avenue,** the trail leads out of the gorge and up to a small grassy area along West River Parkway. Turn to the right, away from the river, and follow the **paved walking path** on the parkway. The path will lead you past the **Lock & Dam #1** site near 46th Street. Follow the walkway as it curves to your right.

Approximately 400 feet from the lock, climb the steep slope at the base of the **46th Street bridge.** You will emerge in **Godfrey Park** on 46th Street as it crosses the Mississippi River. Walk over the bridge and take a left onto **Mississippi River Boulevard.** The paved path leads 1.75 miles along the bluff back to the parking area and lookout point that you started from. This last section of the loop gives you great lookout points to the opposite bank and the bottomlands you were just climbing through a few miles back.

Hike Nearby
The brave of heart can descend the gorge on the St. Paul side of the river as well. After taking a left onto Mississippi River Boulevard off of the Ford Parkway bridge, find a footpath that descends the bluff. This part of the bluff is extremely steep and difficult to descend. Practice extreme caution. A packed dirt trail at the bottom of the gorge twists its way back to the parking lot and lookout point.

Directions
From St. Paul, head west on Summit Avenue for 4.5 miles. Park in the Mississippi River Boulevard parking lot at the end of the avenue by the river. The parking lot is open from dawn until dusk.

   Public Transportation: Bus routes 63 and 134 stop at Summit Avenue and Cretin Avenue.

© JAKE KULJU

This overlook from the trailhead gives a clear view of the Lake Street bridge.

HIDDEN FALLS SHORELINE TRAIL

Hidden Falls Regional Park, St. Paul

Best: Waterfalls

Distance: 3.75 miles round-trip

Duration: 2 hours

Elevation Change: 40 feet

Effort: Easy

Trail: Paved, packed turf

Users: Hikers, wheelchair users, leashed dogs

Season: Year-round; cross-country skiing in winter

Passes/Fees: None

Maps: Maps available at www.stpaul.gov

Contact: St. Paul Parks & Recreation, 1313 Hidden Falls Dr., 651/266-6400, www.stpaul.gov, dawn-dusk daily

Enjoy a quiet riverside hike through the floodplain forest of the Mississippi near the confluence of the Minnesota River.

Hidden Falls Regional Park features a stone stairway and falls viewing area built by the Works Progress Administration (WPA) in the 1930s. The spring-fed waterfall that gives the park its name is tucked into a small ravine on the northern side of the park approximately 0.25 mile from the picnic pavilion. The falls feed a beautiful little creek that empties into the nearby Mississippi River.

As wonderful as this park is, it is rarely crowded, even during summer. This shady walk is a cool and quiet way to escape the city.

Start the Hike

Walk toward the picnic pavilion and across an open grassy area toward **Hidden Falls Creek.** Follow the stream up to the falls and you will see the stonework of **the WPA,** which was laid in 1936 and 1937. A large **stone stairway** leads up to a lookout point over the falls. Two large **stone fire rings** sit in the ravine to the left of the trail.

Retrace your steps out of the ravine and take a right on the **packed dirt path** that follows the bottom of the gorge. The trail is level and wide enough for a wheelchair, but a little bumpy in places. The path loops 1.25 miles back to the parking lot, swinging through the floodplain forest, following a stretch of Mississippi shoreline, and crossing the creek as it empties into

These stone steps lead to the top of the river bluffs. Stonework laid by the WPA in the 1930s is found throughout the park.

the river. Whitetail deer, groundhogs, and raccoons call this area home. As in many of the parks and natural areas along the shores of the Mississippi River in the metro area, oak savannas and bottomland forests cluster along the flats at the base of the river bluffs, providing shade and habitat for songbirds and other wildlife.

When you return to the parking lot, cross the driveway and take a right on the **paved trail** that leads farther into the park. You will walk past the boat landing and will more than likely see a few anglers. **Hidden Falls Regional Park** is just below the **Ford Plant Dam** and is a congregating point for local anglers.

From the **boat landing,** the trail leads south and follows the shore of the Mississippi for another 1.25 miles along a stretch of some of the oldest protected shoreline in the city. The gorge area is home to the serene and shady floodplain forest that characterizes this portion of the river.

You eventually come to the **Highway 5 bridge.** Shortly after crossing under the bridge, the trail enters **Crosby Farm Regional Park.** Turn around at the bridge and return along the trail to the parking lot. This area of the park has many small packed dirt and natural turf trails that run parallel to the paved trail. If you're in the mood, branch off of the pavement and explore some of the side paths that wind through the woods.

Hike Nearby

You can climb out of the bottomlands to get a better view of the opposite shore and the bluff line. Just continue following the paved trail under the Highway 5 bridge and walk up the driveway on your left to Mississippi River Boulevard. Return to the park entrance on the trail high above the river gorge with occasional glimpses of the opposite shore and limestone formations along the face of the bluffs.

Directions

From St. Paul, head west on Shepard Road/Mississippi River Boulevard for 6.5 miles. Take a sharp left down the steep driveway to the north park entrance and parking lot.

Public Transportation: Bus route 46 stops at Cleveland Avenue and Magoffin Avenue.

13 CROSBY FARM LOOP
Crosby Farm Regional Park, St. Paul

Best: Views

Distance: 4.2 miles round-trip

Duration: 2.25 hours

Elevation Change: 50 feet

Effort: Easy/moderate

Trail: Paved, packed turf, gravel

Users: Hikers, wheelchair users, leashed dogs

Season: Year-round; cross-country skiing in winter

Passes/Fees: None

Maps: Maps available at www.stpaul.gov

Contact: St. Paul Parks & Recreation, 2595 Crosby Farm Rd., 651/266-6400, www.stpaul.gov, dawn-dusk daily

---

St. Paul's largest natural park, Crosby Farm, is full of wildflowers, floodplain forest, river vistas, and limestone bluffs.

Comprising 500 acres, Crosby Farm is the largest natural park within the city. It is also one of the state's significant natural areas along the State of Minnesota Mississippi River Critical Area Corridor and the Mississippi National River and Recreation Area.

The park includes two lakes, shares nearly 7 miles of hiking trails with adjacent Hidden Falls Regional Park, and has a sheltered picnic area with restrooms. It displays some of the best-preserved pre-European settlement habitat along the river in the metro area. The park is sandwiched between the Mississippi River and Mississippi River Boulevard/Shepard Road, which run along the bluff that rises from the floodplain.

Start the Hike
From the parking lot at the **Two Rivers Overlook,** take a moment and walk to the viewing area. From the bluff, you can see portions of Fort Snelling State Park, including Pike Island. The overlook shows the confluence of the Minnesota and Mississippi Rivers. From the overlook, walk down **Crosby Farm Road** to your left. The road leads to the **picnic shelter** and open recreation field. A **paved trail** leads

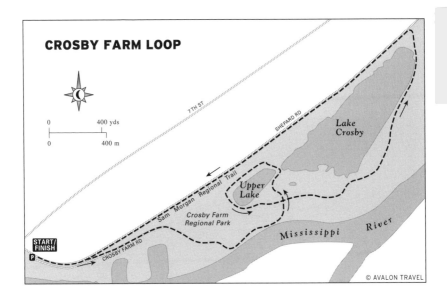

from the shelter toward the river. Follow this path through the floodplain forest and along the banks of the river on the southern end of the park. It is just short of a mile from the overlook to the point where the trail borders the river. This portion of the trail is flush with the water. Anglers commonly fish here at the water's edge.

Crosby Farm is a lush, shady natural park. You will find that the paved trail is excellently maintained, but the rest of the park is mostly natural area with little structural interference. Whitetail deer and great blue herons are commonly found in this expansive floodplain area.

The trail hugs the shore for 0.25 mile and then turns north toward **Upper Lake.** As you walk north, you cross over another paved path that leads east and west. Keep walking straight ahead and **loop counterclockwise** around Upper Lake, crossing the floating boardwalk near the fishing pier. Keep your eyes open for spring ephemeral flowers like bloodroot and trout lily. A study conducted by city officials revealed that more than 300 plant species grow in the park.

As the trail winds around the lake, it eventually becomes the path that you previously crossed. From the crossing point, continue east for another mile along the shore of **Lake Crosby.** Here the trail runs along the shade-filled wooded bottomlands between the lake and the river. As the trail draws closer to the lake, the marshes and low wetlands near the water dominate the scenery. Here you may see some of the huge original cottonwoods that once enjoyed larger numbers along this stretch of the river.

At the northeast end of Lake Crosby, the trail emerges at **Mississippi River Boulevard/Shepard Road.** Take a left here along the paved trail that runs along

© JAKE KULJU

The wetlands of Crosby Farm Regional Park extend for 500 acres along the shore of the Mississippi River.

the upper edge of the bluff. The **bluff line** outlines the northern edge of the entire park for 1.75 miles, revealing beautiful vistas of the opposite shore and the Minnesota and Mississippi River confluence. The trail eventually merges with Crosby Farm Road and leads back to the Two Rivers Overlook point and parking lot.

Extend the Hike

After returning to the Two Rivers Overlook, continue ahead on the paved walkway along Mississippi River Boulevard; 200 feet to your left, the South Entrance to Hidden Falls Regional Park leads down into the floodplain. Follow the road down and take a left onto the paved trail at the bottom of the drive for more riverfront views. The trail leads to the pavilion in Crosby Farm Regional Park. From there, turn left and climb the road that leads back up to the Two Rivers Overlook parking area. This adds 0.25 mile to your hike.

Directions

From St. Paul, head west on Shepard Road, which turns into Mississippi River Boulevard for 5.1 miles. Turn left at Gannon Road onto Crosby Farm Road and Two Rivers Overlook parking area.

Public Transportation: Bus route 54 stops at West 7th Street and Davern Street.

HARRIET ISLAND TO CHEROKEE BLUFFS

Harriet Island Park, St. Paul

Distance: 4.25 miles round-trip

Duration: 2.5-3 hours

Elevation Change: 200 feet

Effort: Moderate/strenuous

Trail: Paved, gravel, packed turf

Users: Hikers, leashed dogs

Season: Year-round; snowshoeing and ice climbing in winter

Passes/Fees: None

Maps: Maps available at www.stpaul.gov

Contact: St. Paul Parks & Recreation, 200 Doctor Justus Ohage Blvd., 651/266-6400, www.stpaul.gov, 6am-10pm daily

---

This challenging hike climbs bluffs, tours fossil beds, and circles Harriet Island Park.

Harriet Island is one of the best-known islands on the Mississippi River, and certainly the one best known to Twin Cities residents. Harriet Island was a true island until 1950, when the channel separating it from the riverbank was filled in. Since then, the city has used it as a public park and annual summer concert grounds.

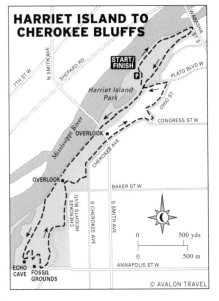

Start the Hike

From the West Entrance parking lot, follow the **paved path** in a **clockwise** direction around the island toward the nearby pavilion. On the way there, you will see the shell of a replica of **Bishop's schoolhouse** near the Harriet Bishop Playground on your right. This stretch of trail leads along the waterfront toward the riverboats docked at **Lower Harbor.** Halfway to the harbor, an **overlook** gives a great river-level view of downtown St. Paul. Continuing, you will walk near the Wabasha Street bridge, get a view of Raspberry Island, and get up close to the historic riverboats, including the **Minnesota Centennial Riverboat.**

Walk along the path as it leads away from the Wabasha Street bridge. The open oak savanna of the park will be to your right as you walk along **Water Street** past the band shell and the pedestrian gateway entrance of the park. At the West entrance, keep heading west along Water Street. You will pass near **Upper Harbor** and follow the base of the river bluffs that quickly rise on your left.

The paved walkway follows the riverside for 1.5 miles, passing under the **Smith Avenue High Bridge** and entering **Lilydale Park.** The area is an undeveloped floodplain on the inner curve of a river bend. Marsh and wooded areas mix in this bottomland park, creating a haven for herons, whitetail deer, and wildflowers.

At the entrance to Lilydale, Water Street becomes Lilydale Road and veers right. Stay to the left and follow the trail to the fossil beds parking lot on the eastern end of **Pickerel Lake.** The trail becomes a **crushed limestone path** that meanders along the base of the bluff on the eastern edge of the park. This trail leads through the floodplain to the foot of the bluff that rises to **Cherokee Park.** The limestone path winds through three switchbacks up the bluff, approximately 150 feet above.

As you near the bluff, you will see several offshoots of the main trail. These lead into the fossil beds. After you make your first sharp left on the limestone path, an offshoot branches to the right. This path leads 20 feet to **Echo Cave,** an artificial cave once used for mushroom growing and cheese making. The cave entrance is blocked off and is used as a hibernating place for brown bats. Do not attempt to

© JAKE KULJU

Water trickles over hanging moss at the foot of a bluff in Lilydale Park.

enter Echo Cave, but take time to look at the fossil grounds around it. After you return to the main trail, start climbing and look for more offshoots—virtually all of them lead to fossil beds and clay pits.

After climbing the switchbacks, you will encounter a T in the trail on top of the bluff. Take a right to see the **Bruce Vento Overlook** just 50 feet away, and return to take a left into **Cherokee Regional Park.** The gravel trail soon emerges from the wooded area to a paved road. Take a left on **Cherokee Heights Boulevard.** The road is lined with parkland on either side. Keep the road on your right and walk approximately 500 feet through the grassy field to a parking lot. From here, a paved path leads east through **Cherokee Regional Park.**

Many natural-turf and packed-dirt paths lead off of the paved walkway toward the edge of the bluff. Explore some of these to get a beautiful vista of the Mississippi River and downtown St. Paul from the bluff top. You will hike the entire length of the park for 1.5 miles, crossing the **Smith Avenue High Bridge** and winding down the bluff slope along Ohio Street. At the bottom of the hill, cross **Plato Boulevard** to the entrance to Harriet Island Park, where you started.

Extend the Hike

To put another mile into this hike, you can cross the Mississippi River along the Smith Avenue High Bridge. The bridge has pedestrian walkways on either side and gives a great view of the river as it winds through downtown. Return on the opposite side of the bridge and continue to Harriet Island.

Directions

From St. Paul, head 0.25 mile south across the Wabasha Street Bridge. Take a right on Water Street and another right into Harriet Island Park at the West Entrance into the parking lot.

Public Transportation: The 75F bus route stops at Wabasha Street and Water Street. A METRO Green Line light rail station is at Union Depot.

15 INDIAN MOUNDS LOOP
Indian Mounds Park, St. Paul

Distance: 1.75 miles round-trip

Duration: 1 hour

Elevation Change: 75 feet

Effort: Easy

Trail: Paved, sidewalk, gravel

Users: Hikers, leashed dogs

Season: Year-round

Passes/Fees: None

Maps: Maps available at www.stpaul.gov

Contact: St. Paul Parks & Recreation, 10 Mounds Blvd., 651/266-6400, www.stpaul.gov, open 24/7

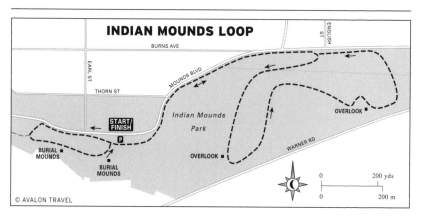

This woodsy walk takes you near ancient Indian burial mounds on bluffs along the Mississippi River.

This peaceful parcel of land is part of the larger Battle Creek Regional Park atop the quiet bluffs of the Mississippi River. As it leaves St. Paul via Pig's Eye Lake, the river carved large limestone cliffs and bluffs that characterize much of the river valley in southern Minnesota.

Start the Hike

From the Mounds Boulevard parking lot, head toward the pavilion on the **paved path** and follow the boulevard for about 700 feet, then veer left toward the river and the edge of the bluff. Stay left at the next two forks in the trail until you come upon the first set of **burial mounds.**

The Minnesota Historical Society has identified six distinct remaining burial mounds and speculates that as many as 37 may have once existed. Approximately 2,000 years old, these mounds are believed to have been left by members of the Hopewell culture.

This section of the park is an open, grassy field with good visibility. The St. Paul skyline is easily spotted, and

This steep trail leads to the blufftop that overlooks the Mississippi River.

benches along the way make this a wonderful spot to take in a summer day.

About 200 feet from the first site, you will come upon **another group of mounds** on your right. Follow the trail to the left back toward the parking lot and follow the paved path east along **Mounds Boulevard.** When you get to **English Street,** turn right and leave the pavement, walking toward the tree line and seven large rocks that mark a trail into the woods. A narrow oak-lined path leads past seasonal streams and ponds. In summer, the plush oaks create a shady canopy over the trail. Wood ducks can be seen here, nesting in houses near the wet areas.

The path eventually veers left up a 30-foot incline to a jutting outlook over **Pig's Eye Lake** and the river valley. A steep, gravelly slope leads down to a trail on the edge of the bluff near **Warner Road.** Turn left at the bottom of the slope and follow the trail along the bottom of a horseshoe-shaped ridge. Take the path near the water. Some fallen trees and branches will be across the trail but can be easily stepped over.

At the opposite point of the horseshoe, the path climbs back up to the ridgeline and another **lookout point.** Take the path as it leads to the left and up another slope into a grouping of Norway pine trees. The trail meets a wider path; take it to the right and follow it back to the **paved path.** Take this left to **Burns Avenue** and it will loop back to the seven large stones. Continue on the paved walkway to the parking lot.

Extend the Hike

You can nearly double the length of this hike by walking west on Mounds Boulevard on the edge of the park to the Bruce Vento Nature Sanctuary and back. The area is a wildlife and native habitat restoration area near the mouth of Lower Phalen Creek.

Directions

From St. Paul, head east on Kellogg Boulevard for 1.3 miles. Turn left on Mounds Boulevard and follow it for 1 mile to the park entrance and Mounds Boulevard parking lot.

Public Transportation: Bus route 70 stops at Burns Avenue and Johnson Parkway.

16 POINT DOUGLAS TRAIL

Battle Creek Regional Park, St. Paul

Distance: 3.5 miles round-trip

Duration: 2 hours

Elevation Change: Negligible

Effort: Easy

Trail: Paved

Users: Hikers, wheelchair users, leashed dogs

Season: Year-round

Passes/Fees: None

Maps: Maps available on the park website

Contact: Ramsey County Parks, 14810 Point Douglas Dr. S., 651/266-8500, www. ramseycounty.us, open 24/7

Follow babbling Battle Creek from the Point Douglas ravine to the park's upper ponds.

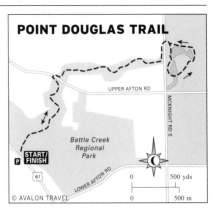

The Battle Creek trail starting at Point Douglas is a beautiful tour of a Mississippi River creek valley tributary. Headed south of St. Paul on Highway 61/10 amid the wrecked car recycling factory and the expansive train yard, you wouldn't think one of the city's most peaceful hikes was nearby. But right off the highway, the short Point Douglas Road leads to just that.

Start the Hike

From the parking lot at the end of the short road, walk through the ravine with the creek on your right. The soft limestone walls are a bright contrast to the dark trees that line the low bluffs of this area. The **paved trail** follows the creek upstream past a series of 10 three-tiered **waterfalls** and as many **footbridges** that crisscross the open water. Benches are placed intermittently along the trail, and open, grassy areas invite picnickers and sunbathers, as well as groups of wild turkeys.

These tiered waterfalls line the creek all the way along the Point Douglas trail.

As the trail leads away from the parking lot, the limestone cliffs meld into pine and oak woodland and some wetland grass near the creek. In 0.75 mile, the path rises to cross **Upper Afton Road/Battle Creek Road.** When you reach the road, take a right and cross to the other side of the creek where the paved trail dips back down to the creek. A third of a mile later, after the seventh waterfall and a grove of pine trees, cross **Ruth Street.**

The creek widens here, slightly, and the footbridges become larger. After the tenth waterfall, the path makes a large S curve and emerges at **McKnight Road.** Cross the road and take a left onto the sidewalk. The paved path will be on your right in 100 yards and will circle through a large portion of the park with three distinct bodies of water. Make a loop around the ponds and the sheltered area. This section of the park is bisected by **Upper Afton Road.** The area is dominated by a majestic oak savanna that provides acres of shaded ground. After walking through the trees and around the ponds, retrace your steps downstream from the shelter, across **McKnight Road,** and back to **Point Douglas.** Since you travel from higher to lower ground on the return trip, there are areas along the trail where you can see far downstream and take in several of the small waterfalls at once. Bring your camera on this hike, as it is one of St. Paul's most picturesque walking trails.

Extend the Hike

If you feel like going all out, continue following the path to your right after crossing McKnight Road. You will cross Upper Afton Road and enter the southern portion of the park. Another mile of trail loops through several more ponds and returns you to the shelter near McKnight Road.

Directions

From St. Paul, head east on Shepard Road/Warner Road for 2.4 miles. Veer right onto U.S. Highway 10 East for 1.5 miles. Turn left at Lower Afton Road and take an immediate left onto Point Douglas Road. Continue to the Point Douglas parking lot.

Public Transportation: Bus routes 361, 364, and 365 stop at Lower Afton Road.

17 BATTLE CREEK LOOP
Battle Creek Regional Park, St. Paul

Distance: 1.5 miles round-trip

Duration: 1 hour

Elevation Change: 80 feet

Effort: Easy

Trail: Paved, packed turf

Users: Hikers, leashed dogs

Season: Year-round; cross-country skiing in winter

Passes/Fees: None

Maps: Maps available on the park website

Contact: Battle Creek Regional Park, 2300 Upper Afton Road, Maplewood, 651/266-8500, www.ramseycounty.us, dawn-dusk daily

This hike explores the eastern section of Battle Creek Regional Park.

Battle Creek Regional Park is one of the largest open spaces in the metro area. Consisting of Battle Creek Lake, the westward-flowing Battle Creek itself, Indian Mounds Park, and Pig's Eye Lake, it is a 1,840-acre Mississippi River Watershed area. The park preserves open and wild areas between the highly developed urban landscape of St. Paul and the suburban community of Woodbury.

BATTLE CREEK LOOP

START/FINISH

S WINTHROP ST

Battle Creek
Regional
Park

LOWER AFTON RD

0   300 yds

0   300 m

© AVALON TRAVEL

Start the Hike

Facing the recreation center, take a left to the trailhead, marked by a **white sign.** A grassy trail leads you to the right of a **small pond.** Wooded areas, grasslands, and wetlands characterize this portion of the park. The beginning of the trail is spotted with pine and large oak trees.

Fifty yards from the trailhead, slant right up a steep hill. This open, grassy area is used for cross-country skiing in the winter. The trail turns left at the top of the hill, but take a moment to turn around and look at the sweeping view of the pond and lower portion of the park.

At the top of the hill, the trail moves into a wooded area. Entering an oak canopy, the trail bends left into a stand of birch trees. Take a right up a small 20-foot slope and take another right at the top. Another 30 feet later, turn left, following the **orange marker arrow.** This is a ridgeline trail above an oak-filled gully. The trail breaks to an open view of the floodplain to the west. Advance to the next **orange marker** on the other side of a grassy meadow. Take a left at the marker onto a narrow tree-root trail down into the gully. When a wider trail merges with yours, stay straight to the next orange marker and take a left into scattered birch trees and a gradual uphill slant.

Natural turf trails run throughout Battle Creek Regional Park.

This portion of the trail borders **Lower Afton Road.** Take a right at the next **orange marker** and another right onto a wide gravel path. Take a left at a small gate and a right at the next **orange marker** to leave the woods and reenter the open grass and pond area near the recreation center. Move to the right along the tree line back to the parking lot.

Extend the Hike

To add another mile to your hike, cross Battle Creek Road at the bottom of the slope you descend after taking a left at the grassy meadow. A trail loops through a smaller wooded section of the park and returns to the same crossing point on the road.

Directions

From St. Paul, head east on I-94 for 3 miles. Exit on White Bear Avenue and take a right. Turn left at Upper Afton Road for 0.8 mile. Turn right at Winthrop Street and right into the Battle Creek Regional Park entrance and parking lot. Parking is easy to find—the recreation center has a large parking lot and excellent facilities.

Public Transportation: Bus routes 361, 364, and 365 stop at Lower Afton Road.

18 THEODORE WIRTH WILDFLOWER TRAIL
Theodore Wirth Regional Park, Golden Valley

Best: Wildflowers

Distance: 2.8 miles round-trip

Duration: 1.5-2 hours

Elevation Change: Negligible

Effort: Easy

Trail: Paved, packed turf

Users: Hikers, cyclists, leashed dogs

Season: Year-round; cross-country skiing in winter

Passes/Fees: None

Maps: Maps available on the park website

Contact: Theodore Wirth Regional Park, 1339 Theodore Wirth Pkwy., 612/230-6400, www.minneapolisparks.org, 6am-midnight daily

---

View the renowned Eloise Butler Wildflower Garden and Bird Sanctuary.

With the Minneapolis skyline just a few miles away, this secluded little forest glen does an amazing job of blocking out the urban landscape and bringing you face to face with some of the rarest and most beautiful native wildflowers in the state.

Start the Hike
The entrance to the garden is adjacent to the parking lot. Walk through the metal gates that start the **garden trail** and follow the 0.5 mile of meandering **wood-chip path** through the displays. Each stand of flowers is identified by a small plaque. You will see trout lilies, bloodroot, and coneflowers, along with dozens of other beautiful wildflowers. Take as many pictures as you'd like, but leave your dog behind. Pets are not allowed in the garden. After winding through the flowers, the trail returns you to the metal gates at the parking lot.

Cross the **park road** and take a left on the **paved trail** that leads south toward **Birch Pond;** 0.25 mile from the parking lot, that trail crosses the park road and runs parallel to Theodore Wirth Parkway. Take a left at **Wayzata Boulevard** and follow the trail up the slight hill into the oak savanna portion of the park.

Take a left 0.5 mile north of Wayzata Boulevard as the paved trail makes its way northwest toward the **picnic area.** Keep to the right at the picnic tables;

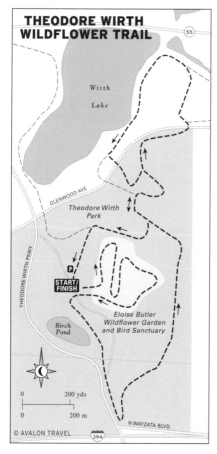

THEODORE WIRTH
WILDFLOWER TRAIL

Wirth
Lake

GLENWOOD AVE

Theodore Wirth
Park

THEODORE WIRTH PKWY

P

START/
FINISH

Birch
Pond

Eloise Butler
Wildflower Garden
and Bird Sanctuary

0   200 yds
0   200 m

N WAYZATA BLVD

© AVALON TRAVEL   394

then take another right at the trail T. This path arcs north to another **picnic area** in a grassy clearing. Follow the path as it parallels **Glenwood Avenue,** and then cross the road and veer left across the **bike trail.** The path makes a 0.5-mile loop around the **Wirth Lake picnic area,** passing the boat landing and the Beach House. Take a left at the **Beach House** and cross the bike trail and Glenwood Avenue toward the first picnic area. Turn right at the next two trail intersections through the oaks, and then take a left 0.3 mile from the picnic area to return to the wildflower garden parking lot and trailhead.

Extend the Hike

You can spend more time near the water by taking a right just after crossing Glenwood Avenue the first time. The paved path leads east for 0.5 mile past the JD Rivers' Children's Garden and then swings northwest along Bassett's Creek for another 0.5 mile. The trail merges with the picnic area loop near Wirth Lake and brings you past the boat landing to the Beach House. This adds 1 mile to your hike and gives you some walking time along the shores of a peaceful, tree-lined creek.

Directions

From Minneapolis, head west on MN Highway 55 for 2.3 miles. Turn left onto Theodore Wirth Parkway for 0.5 mile. After crossing Glenwood Avenue, take a left into the Eloise Butler Wildflower Garden parking lot.

BRAINERD LAKES AND THE MISSISSIPPI RIVER VALLEY

© JAKE KULJU

This diverse area is rich in history and habitat. Hiking terrain can be separated into three sections: hardwood and evergreen forests and marshy wetlands in the north; open, rolling prairie lands extending west toward the Dakotas; and the floodplain forests north of Minneapolis. Many Dakota villages and early European settlements took root along the river and surrounding plains and forests. Archaeological digs in Mille Lacs Kathio State Park revealed signs of Native American villages more than 9,000 years old. The confluence of the Crow Wing and Mississippi Rivers, once the site of a logging and trading town, still holds the Beaulieu House mansion. Find the boyhood home and practice fields of aviator Charles Lindbergh at his namesake state park. Farther south are the winding oxbows and floodplain forests of the Rum River. River trails lead past abandoned barns, through canoe campsites, and along transitional zones between forest and field.

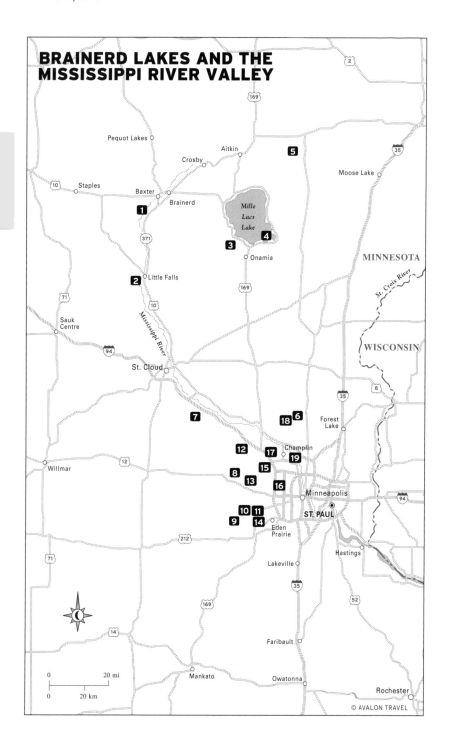

BRAINERD LAKES AND THE MISSISSIPPI RIVER VALLEY

	TRAIL NAME	LEVEL	DISTANCE	TIME	ELEVATION	PAGE
1	Crow Wing Confluence Trail	Moderate	6.2 mi rt	3.5 hr	60 ft	74
2	Charles A. Lindbergh Hiking Club Trail	Easy	3.4 mi rt	1.5-2 hr	100 ft	77
3	Mille Lacs Loop	Easy	3.1 mi rt	1.5-2 hr	30 ft	79
4	Mille Lacs Shoreline Trail	Easy	2.5 mi rt	1.5 hr	Negligible	82
5	Rice Lake Refuge Trail	Easy	3 mi rt	1.5 hr	Negligible	85
6	Mount Tom Trail	Easy/moderate	3.7 mi rt	2 hr	100 ft	87
7	Big Woods Loop	Easy	3.6 mi rt	2 hr	70 ft	89
8	Lake Rebecca Loop	Easy/moderate	3.5 mi rt	2.5-3 hr	50 ft	91
9	Crosby Lake Trail	Easy/moderate	4 mi rt	2-2.5 hr	50 ft	93
10	Lundsten Lake Loop	Easy/moderate	4.8 mi rt	2.5 hr	Negligible	96
11	Minnetonka Trail	Easy	1 mile rt	0.5-1 hr	Negligible	98
12	Crow River Loop	Moderate	5.7 mi rt	3 hr	50 ft	100
13	Lake Katrina Loop	Easy/moderate	5.5 mi rt	2.5-3 hr	Negligible	103
14	Lake Minnewashta and Woodland Loop Trails	Easy	2.65 mi rt	2 hr	30 ft	105
15	Fish Lake Trail	Easy	2.6 mi rt	1.5 hr	30 ft	107
16	Medicine Lake Trail	Easy	1.5 mi rt	1 hr	40 ft	109
17	Elm Creek Trail	Easy/moderate	4.75 mi rt	3 hr	Negligible	111
18	Rum River Trail	Easy	3.25 mi rt	1.5 hr	50 ft	114
19	Coon Rapids Dam Trail	Easy	2.7 mi rt	1-1.5 hr	Negligible	116

1 CROW WING CONFLUENCE TRAIL

Crow Wing State Park, Brainerd

Best: River Hikes, Viewing Wildlife

Distance: 6.2 miles round-trip

Duration: 3.5 hours

Elevation Change: 60 feet

Effort: Moderate

Trail: Packed turf

Users: Hikers, leashed dogs

Season: April-October; snowshoeing in winter

Passes/Fees: $5 daily vehicle permit fee

Maps: Maps available at the park office and on the park website

Contact: Crow Wing State Park, 3124 State Park Road, 218/825-3075, www. dnr.state.mn.us, 8am-10pm daily

View the historic sites at the wooded confluence of the Mississippi and Crow Wing Rivers.

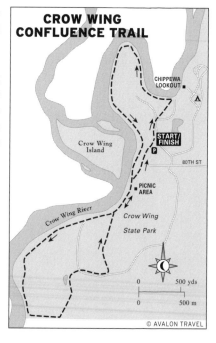

Just south of Brainerd, Crow Wing State Park is on the northern edge of the Mississippi River Sand Plains region, which was formed by the outwash from the giant glacial Lake Grantsburg.

Start the Hike

The trail begins directly west of the parking lot near the **missionary chapel.** Take a right onto the path and head north for 0.3 mile toward the **boat landing.** When you reach the boat landing, take a hard left at the parking lot along the southern shore of the Mississippi River's oxbow.

© JAKE KULJU

An alert chipmunk holds still on a fallen tree branch.

At the next trail intersection, 0.2 mile ahead, stay to the right and follow a portion of the **Red River Oxcart Trail** as it drops 30 feet into the floodplain and arcs around the peninsula of land that juts into the oxbow. The trees are broken into clusters where patches of meadow have taken hold here. Stay to the right at the next two trail intersections before reaching the **Beaulieu House historic site.**

Continue south for 0.2 mile back into the thick pine, maple, oak, and aspen forest to the picnic area parking lot, staying to the right as the trail continues south up the riverbank and through the **picnic area;** 0.3 mile from the picnic area, stay to the right at the trail intersection.

Continue west along the riverside trail past the **canoe camp.** Stay right at the next trail intersection and walk past the **G1 group campsite.** Continue south for 1.5 miles to the southern border of the park, where the trail makes a 90-degree bend to the east. The trees become less dense once more, with swaths of meadow brushed on the landscape. Some prairie flowers may line the trail here in spring. This transitional zone is a haven for wildlife. Whitetail deer, badgers, raccoons, foxes, and even coyotes live here. Porcupines also love the tall pine trees.

Veer left at the next **two trail intersections.** The trail makes a small eastern arc for 0.1 mile and then meets a T. Turn right and then left in 0.2 mile to walk north to the intersection just north of the **rifle pits.** Take a right at the end of the 0.6-mile stretch of trail and retrace your steps back through the picnic area. Take a right at the picnic area parking lot to the chapel at the trailhead and parking lot.

Extend the Hike

At the boat landing, take a right and climb 40 feet to Chippewa Lookout, a pine-tree-clad hill above the shores of the Mississippi that gives a stunning view of the waterway. This short diversion adds only 0.2 mile to your hike. The overlook point presides over the large oxbow the river makes before it reaches Crow Wing Island. This is also an excellent viewing point for eagles and hawks. On sunny days you can see for miles.

Directions

From Minneapolis, take I-94 West for 63 miles. Exit onto MN 15 North toward St. Cloud for another 9 miles. Take U.S. Highway 10 West for 29 miles; then merge onto MN 371 North for 20 miles. Turn left at Koering Road for 0.2 mile and continue straight onto County Road 27. Go straight past the park office to the parking lot by the picnic area.

2 CHARLES A. LINDBERGH HIKING CLUB TRAIL
Charles A. Lindbergh State Park, Little Falls

Distance: 3.4 miles round-trip

Duration: 1.5-2 hours

Elevation Change: 100 feet

Effort: Easy

Trail: Gravel, packed turf

Users: Hikers, leashed dogs

Season: April-October; snowshoeing in winter

Passes/Fees: $5 daily vehicle permit fee

Maps: Maps available at the park office and on the park website

Contact: Charles A. Lindbergh State Park, 1615 Lindbergh Drive South, 320/616-2525, www.dnr.state.mn.us, 8am-10pm daily

---

Hike amid beautiful views of the upper Mississippi River.

The rising river bluffs and grassland prairie that blanket this area make for a beautiful hike.

Start the Hike
From the picnic area parking lot, follow the **Hiking Club trail** west toward **Pike Creek.** This park is known for its massive red pine trees, and you'll soon see why. The stately pines hearken back to the time when much of this area and the entire northeastern section of the state were covered in thick pine forest. The path crosses the creek in 0.1 mile and then splits. Turn right and make the ascent up the creek valley to start the **counterclockwise Hiking Club trail loop;** 0.2 mile from the creek, take a right at the trail intersection. Just a few hundred feet ahead is an overlook point above the vista of the creek valley. Keep walking north through the thick red pine and oak forest landscape for 0.5 mile as the trail parallels Pike Creek and makes a gentle descent. This northern arc of the trail is across the creek from the campground in the thick forest.

The top of the trail meets an intersecting path that forms a T. Take a left and head south 0.6 mile away from the creek through the wide meadow. Keep to the right at the next trail intersection. The trail dives back into the forest here as

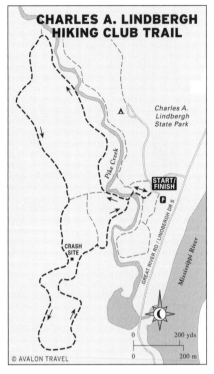

it moves south; 0.2 mile from the last intersection, the trail passes the crash **landing site of Lindbergh's Jenny plane.** A small spur trail leads to the clearing in the trees, memorialized by a **plaque.** Return to the main trail and take a right along the 1-mile arc that leads up and over a small ridge and back north to the **overlook point.**

At the end of the 1-mile arc, take a right and follow the Hiking Club trail 0.3 mile northeast back to the **Pike Creek bridge.** Take a right after crossing the bridge back to the park road that leads to the trailhead and picnic area parking lot.

Shorten the Hike

A trail at the upper end of the Hiking Club trail loop crosses back over Pike Creek and passes through the camping area. This option shortens the hike to a more peaceful 1.6-mile creek-side walk. After walking to the creek, take a right before crossing and follow the trail north through the Pike Creek valley to the campground. Take a left at the group camp driveway and take a right 0.2 mile later at the next trail intersection. The trail arcs south to the eastern edge of the campground and then follows the park road south back to the parking lot and trailhead.

Directions

From Minneapolis, take I-94 West for 63 miles. Exit onto MN 15 North toward St. Cloud for another 9 miles. Take U.S. Highway 10 West for 25 miles, then exit onto County Road 76 North toward Little Falls for 2.8 miles. Turn left at MN 27 and left again onto County Road 52 for 1.5 miles. Take a right at the park entrance and follow signs to the Charles A. Lindbergh State Park parking lot near the picnic area.

❸ MILLE LACS LOOP

Mille Lacs Kathio State Park, Onamia

🖼 🖼 🖼 🖼

Best: Historical Hikes

Distance: 3.1 miles round-trip

Duration: 1.5-2 hours

Elevation Change: 30 feet

Effort: Easy

Trail: Packed turf, gravel

Users: Hikers, leashed dogs

Season: April-October; cross-country skiing in winter

Passes/Fees: $5 daily vehicle permit fee

Maps: Maps available at the park office and on the park website

Contact: Mille Lacs Kathio State Park, 15066 Kathio State Park Road, 320/532-3523, www.dnr.state.mn.us, 8am-10pm daily

---

View ancient Native American sites.

Evidence of Native American villages in what is now Mille Lacs Kathio State Park dates back more than 9,000 years. You can actually see signs of where and how people—first the Dakota and then the Ojibwe tribes—recognized it for its abundant natural wealth.

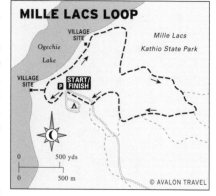

Start the Hike

Begin at the trailhead just south of the parking lot. Follow the packed **dirt trail** as it makes a quick northward hook and comes to a T about 0.2 mile from the trailhead. Turn left onto a branch trail that leads you through an **archaeological dig site.** When the trail reconnects with the main path, take a right. The next village site is about 0.5 mile to the north along the shore of Ogechie Lake.

Veer left down to the lakeshore at the **second village site.** Continue north and climb 15 feet or so back up to the trail. In another 0.1 mile, the trail hooks south and enters the wooded, hilly portion of this hike.

© JAKE KULJU

Native Americans have lived on or near Ogechie Lake for more than 9,000 years.

As you move away from Ogechie Lake, you become connected to a network of hiking trails that crisscross throughout this rich, wooded area of the park. Continue following the **Hiking Club signs,** which point you in the right direction at each trail intersection. This thick-canopied oak and maple forest area is characterized by gently rolling hills and pockets of marshy wetland areas in the low places.

About 1 mile from Ogechie Lake at **numbered post 14,** make a sharp right and head west along the Hiking Club trail toward the parking lot. You are just past the halfway point of the hike. The forest turf trail continues through thick woods until it emerges on the road that leads to the parking lot. Take a right and follow the gravel road north. From here, you are 0.2 mile from the trailhead.

Hikes Nearby

Mille Lacs Kathio is full of trails and historic sites. Drive and park at the picnic area at the southern end of Lake Ogechie to get access to several more miles of hiking trails, the Ogechie dam, and another historic Native American site near the park's interpretive center. From the parking lot, follow the trail that leads west from the picnic area to the historic marker at the dam. Return to the parking lot and walk north, and then turn right onto the hiking trail that leads east for 0.5 mile past the camper cabins and arcs north to another trail loop in the center of the park. From here, you can take a right toward the lookout tower, a left to Ogechie Campground, or turn around and walk back to the picnic area parking lot.

Directions

From Minneapolis, drive north on I-35 West for 3 miles. Merge onto U.S. Highway 10 West for 23 miles. Exit onto U.S. Highway 169 North for 63 miles. Turn left at Shakopee Lake Road and take a right onto Kathio State Park Road. Drive another 2 miles past the park entrance to the Ogechie Campground and Landmark Trail parking lot.

4 MILLE LACS SHORELINE TRAIL
Father Hennepin State Park, Isle

Distance: 2.5 miles round-trip

Duration: 1.5 hours

Elevation Change: Negligible

Effort: Easy

Trail: Paved, packed turf, gravel

Users: Hikers, leashed dogs

Season: April-October; snowshoeing in winter

Passes/Fees: $5 daily vehicle permit fee

Maps: Maps available at the park office and on the park website

Contact: Father Hennepin State Park, 41294 Father Hennepin Park Road, 320/676-8763, www.dnr.state.mn.us, 8am-10pm daily

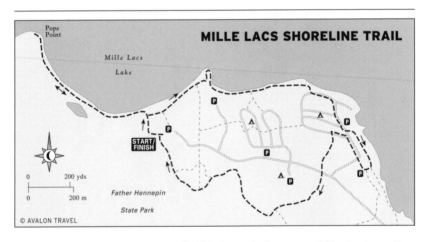

Explore the southern shore of Mille Lacs Lake, one of the last nesting places of the common tern.

This quiet lakeshore hike along one of Minnesota's largest bodies of water is just over an hour and a half from Minneapolis.

Start the Hike
The trailhead begins on the western edge of the parking lot. The **gravel path** arcs

Maple and birch trees provide a shady path along the rocky shore of Mille Lacs Lake.

north to a picnic area on the southern shore of the lake. Take a left here toward Pope Point. The 0.5-mile path to the point hugs the rocky shore of **Mille Lacs Lake** and treats you to beautiful vistas of the water and distant shore. When you reach **Pope Point,** an information kiosk provides information about the rare common tern. The unique boulder habitat of Mille Lacs Lake supplies the specific nesting and feeding habitat the tern needs to survive. Backtrack to the picnic area where you turned left and continue following the shoreline east. This 0.1 mile leads past the beach and **picnic areas** of the park. Just before the **boat launch,** a spur trail to your left makes a quick loop on a small point. Venture out to the point for another view of mighty Mille Lacs.

When you rejoin the trail, you will enter a thick maple grove, creating a shady, almost enchanted forest feeling. Whitetail deer, foxes, and other smaller creatures can be spotted here, or at least signs of them. A short 0.2 mile from the maple grove, you come upon **Lakeview Campground.** The trail follows the campground road for 0.1 mile. Take a right before reaching the boat landing and walk past the playground and parking area. Walk past the first sign on your left for the **Hiking Club trail** and take the next right. About 500 feet down this path, take a left into red and white pine forest. This forest turf trail leads south, away from the lake, and is lined with tall, whispering pine trees. The path crosses the park road and arcs east. Turn right at the next trail intersection in 0.5 mile. At the third map kiosk you encounter, veer left on the Hiking Club trail, staying to your left at each of the next two intersections. From the fourth map kiosk, the trailhead is 0.1 mile away. From here, make a short right turn back to the parking lot.

Extend the Hike

Instead of doubling back at the eastern picnic area on the Hiking Club trail, you can continue straight on a 0.5-mile trail that links to the Hiking Club trail about 0.5 mile before returning to the trailhead. While this detour doesn't add significant distance to your hike, it takes you deeper into the quiet pine woods of this peaceful park and increases your chances of seeing wildlife.

Directions

From Minneapolis, drive north on I-35 West for 3 miles. Merge onto U.S. Highway 10 West for 23 miles. Exit onto U.S. Highway 169 North for 63 miles. Turn left, following the state park sign for 0.3 mile. Take a right into the park entrance. Follow signs to the beach area parking lot.

5 RICE LAKE REFUGE TRAIL
Rice Lake National Wildlife Refuge, McGregor

Distance: 3 miles round-trip

Duration: 1.5 hours

Elevation Change: Negligible

Effort: Easy

Trail: Packed turf, gravel

Users: Hikers, leashed dogs

Season: April-October; snowshoeing in winter

Passes/Fees: None

Maps: Maps available at the park headquarters and on the park website

Contact: Rice Lake National Wildlife Refuge, 36298 MN 65, 218/768-2402, www.fws.gov/midwest/ricelake

Hike through one of the continent's major bird migration corridors.

The Rice Lake National Wildlife Refuge (RLNWR) is one of the most important stops for birds along North America's central bird migration corridor. This refuge is a must-visit in the spring and fall months when birds such as the American coot, ruby-throated hummingbird, and belted kingfisher are on the move.

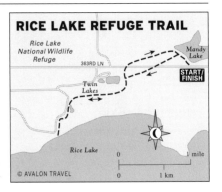

Start the Hike
Follow the south shore of **Mandy Lake** as the trail leads you west toward **North Bog Road;** 0.5 mile from the trailhead, veer left at the intersection. After walking through the red pine and oak forest, you will shortly break into an open field just before the **CCC Camp parking lot.** To the south is a wide bog area.

Continue east from the parking lot for 0.25 mile to the next open field and trail intersection. Take a left here onto the **Rice Lake Pool trail.** This path leads through the tallgrass and wetland areas surrounding Rice Lake and ends at the

Wild mushrooms grow on the forest floor in Rice Lake National Wildlife Refuge.

observation tower on the reedy northern shore. This area is rich with nesting and feeding waterfowl, especially during the migratory seasons.

Follow the Rice Lake Pool trail back to the CCC Camp parking lot and take a left, returning to Mandy Lake on the northern arm of the small loop. After taking a right at the trail intersection near the water, you are 0.50 mile from the trailhead and parking lot.

Extend the Hike

On the return trip from the Rice Lake observation tower, take a left at the first trail intersection. This detour takes you past the Twin Lakes and along the northern edge of the grassy area near the trailhead, reconnecting at Mandy Lake and adding 0.75 mile to your hike.

Directions

From St. Paul, head north on I-35 East for 87 miles. Exit on MN 73 toward Moose Lake. Turn left at MN 73 for 2.5 miles, and left again onto MN 27/MN 73 for another 5 miles. Stay left on MN 27 for 19 miles and turn right onto MN 65; 5 miles north, take a left into the Rice Lake National Wildlife Refuge. Drive 2 miles past the headquarters building and park at the Mandy Lake parking lot.

6 MOUNT TOM TRAIL
Sibley State Park, New London

Distance: 3.7 miles round-trip

Duration: 2 hours

Elevation Change: 100 feet

Effort: Easy/moderate

Trail: Paved, packed turf

Users: Hikers, cyclists, leashed dogs

Season: April-October; cross-country skiing in winter

Passes/Fees: $5 state park vehicle permit fee

Maps: Maps available at the park headquarters and on the park website

Contact: Sibley State Park, 800 Sibley Park Road NE, 320/354-2055, www.dnr.state.mn.us, 8am-10pm daily

View the rolling hills, lush hardwood forests, and hilltop prairies from atop Mount Tom.

Retreating glaciers sculpted the Sibley State Park area during the last ice age. This hike meanders through hills, tallgrass prairie, and thick forest.

Start the Hike
Facing the **Trail Center,** you will find the trailhead to your left. Keep to the left at the first intersection, just 0.2 mile up the trail along the edge of the oak forest. At the second junction, take another left onto the **Mount Tom Trail** toward Lake Andrew.

On its way to Lake Andrew, the trail crosses a park road and a paved bike path as well as a shared-use hiker/cyclist path. Stay on the turf trail and turn right at the lakeshore, following the water for 0.3 mile. The **lakeside trail** merges with the paved biking trail and shared-use trail but shortly breaks off to the right. Follow this turf trail north for 0.3 mile through the maple, oak, and aspen trees; then take a left to continue on the Mount Tom Trail. From the lake, the trail ascends to grassy **Badger Hill.** Take a left on the short spur trail that leads to the Badger Hill overlook 0.4 mile from the last trail intersection.

Return to the **Mount Tom Trail** and take a left back down the hill and through the forest. Turn right at the next intersection and walk 0.4 mile to the park road. Take a left and follow the road west for a few hundred feet; then turn right at the sign pointing to the Mount Tom Trail. **Little Mount Tom** lies just 0.1 mile

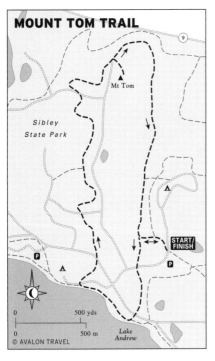

northeast in an elevated forest clearing. Keep going for 0.2 mile to the gravel parking lot at the foot of Mount Tom. Walk to the eastern end of the parking lot and take a right at the trail intersection. This path leads up 60 feet to the stone tower atop the hill. Climb the several dozen steps to the top of the **overlook tower** for a sweeping view on all sides of the hills, forests, farmland, and meadows of the area.

Return to the parking lot and take a right on the trail that leads north through the trees. As the trail arcs south, it rolls up and down with the undulating, wooded hills. Take a left at the trail intersection 1.2 miles from Mount Tom that leads back to the trailhead. Keep to the right at the next one, just 0.1 mile east. The parking lot lies 0.2 mile away along the oak and grassland transitional zone where you started the hike.

Extend the Hike

If 3.7 miles isn't enough for you, take a left at the first intersection 0.9 mile after Mount Tom. A trail makes a 1.1-mile circle through the thick forest that surrounds the campground area. After passing the overlook point 1 mile from the trail intersection, turn right to return to the parking lot and trailhead at the Trail Center.

Directions

From Minneapolis, head west on I-94 for 2.3 miles. Take the I-394 West exit and keep right at the fork. I-394 merges with U.S. Highway 12 West in 8 miles. Continue west on U.S. Highway 12 for 81.7 miles. Turn right onto the U.S. Highway 71 East ramp and merge onto U.S. Highway 71 for 13 miles. Turn left at Sibley Park Road for 1.2 miles to the park entrance. Take the next two right turns after the park office for 0.3 mile, following signs to the Trail Center parking lot.

7 BIG WOODS LOOP
Lake Maria State Park, Monticello

Distance: 3.6 miles round-trip

Duration: 2 hours

Elevation Change: 70 feet

Effort: Easy

Trail: Mowed path, packed turf

Users: Hikers, leashed dogs

Season: April-October; cross-country skiing in winter

Passes/Fees: $5 state park vehicle permit fee

Maps: Maps available at the park headquarters and on the park website

Contact: Lake Maria State Park, 11411 Clementa Avenue NE, 763/878-2325, www.dnr.state.mn.us, 8am-10pm daily

Hike over Anderson Hill and around Lake Maria.

This wilderness hike is only a 45-minute drive from the Twin Cities.

Start the Hike

The **Trail Center** is about 300 feet west of the parking lot. Start here and take a left onto the **Big Woods Loop trail.** Wooden signs with arrows are placed at most trail intersections, including the Trail Center. A quarter mile into the hike, the trail makes a sharp left into open grassland. Walk straight ahead on the mowed pathway and across the road you drove on near the park entrance.

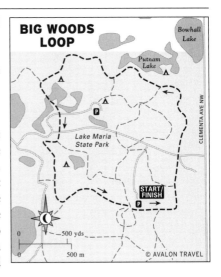

As the trail curves to the left, it hugs the foot of **Anderson Hill,** one of the highest points in the park. A lone tree grows atop the hill, but it's a steep 40-foot scramble to get there. Follow the trail down the other side of the hill into the woods. This is the beginning of the **Big Woods forest** the trail is named after.

This gnarly maple stands out from the rest of the Big Woods forest in Lake Maria State Park.

The next 0.25 mile takes you past three hike-in campsites along **Putnam Lake.** This is a low, wetland area, and in the spring it can be a little mucky. Just past the trail to **Camper Cabin C-1** (you'll see a sign for it), there is an information sign at a trail intersection. The main trail seems to go left, but you want to stay to your right on the **Big Woods Loop trail.** If you enter a group campsite, you'll know you went the wrong way.

The forest turf trail continues to wind through large basswoods and shady maple trees. Near the 2-mile mark, the trail makes a T. A footpath to the right leads to Lake Maria; take the wider **Big Woods Loop,** which turns left. The following 0.5 mile leads you past the **B-5 campsite,** C-2 camper cabin paths, across a low-lying pond and wetland area, and then across two of the park's gravel roads. At the second crossing, the trail reenters the forest about 200 feet up the road on your left.

Shortly after leaving the road, the trail meets another T. Take a right and oxbow around a small hill through the rolling forest turf trail in the thick of the Big Woods. A half mile after the T, take a left following signs for the Big Woods Loop and **Bjorkland Lake Trail.** In just under 0.5 mile, you'll be back at the Trail Center and parking lot.

Extend the Hike

Just before the B-5 campsite, take a right on the 0.5-mile trail that leads past Lake Maria to the Zunnbrunnen Interpretive Trail. Adding a total of 1 mile to your hike, this option gives you a view of the park's namesake lake and takes you across a boardwalk through a marsh to the interpretive trail.

Directions

From Minneapolis, head west on I-94 for 37 miles. Exit onto MN 25 toward Monticello and turn right for 0.5 mile. Turn left at West Broadway Street and left on Elm Street 0.5 mile later. Turn right onto County Road 39 for 5.5 miles and take another right onto County Road 111. The park entrance is 0.5 mile on your left. Follow signs to the Trail Center parking lot.

8 LAKE REBECCA LOOP

Lake Rebecca Park Reserve, Greenfield

Best: Viewing Wildlife

Distance: 3.5 miles round-trip

Duration: 2.5-3 hours

Elevation Change: 50 feet

Effort: Easy/moderate

Trail: Forest turf, gravel road

Users: Hikers, cyclists, leashed dogs

Season: April-October

Passes/Fees: None

Maps: Map available on the park website

Contact: Lake Rebecca Park Reserve, 9831 County Road 50, 763/694-7860, www.threeriversparks.org, 5am-10pm daily April-October, closed November-March

---

This hike traverses prairie hills and lakeside ridges.

Tucked into a bend of the twisting Crow River, Lake Rebecca Park Reserve is an undeveloped lake surrounded by Big Woods forest and prairie.

Start the Hike

Facing the lake at the paved boat launch just north of the parking lot, follow the **forest turf trail** to your right; 500 feet from the trailhead, take the trail leading to your left and climb 20 feet to the **ridge above Lake Rebecca's western shore.** The trail leads south along the shore and gives you glimpses of the lake's bright blue waters through the trees. A quarter mile from the intersection, a **scenic overlook** opens to the west over a pond and low-lying area that is home to one of the state's largest flocks of trumpeter swans.

The trail soon leaves the lake and begins carving through the undulating prairie landscape. Just before it does, it crosses a **paved bike path** and does so again in another 0.5 mile.

Just 500 feet after the **second bike path** crossing, the trail follows a **park service road** for another 500 feet. Turn left at the intersection and turn right back onto the prairie trail. Near the pond, the trail meets the park service road again.

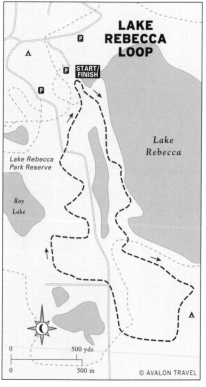

This loop shares use with mountain bikes, so watch for oncoming riders. It is a one-way clockwise loop for bikers, so you'll know where they will be coming from. From the pond, the trailhead lies 0.3 mile to the northeast. Cross the service road and take a left at the intersection back to the paved boat landing. Straight ahead is the small hill that leads up to the ridge above the lake.

Shorten the Hike

For a shortcut through the prairie grasses and wildflowers, take a right on the paved biking trail that leads away from the lake 0.2 mile south of the overlook point. The trail leads west for just under 0.5 mile until it crosses the unpaved, grassy hiking path again. Take a right to continue on the loop as it heads north along the service road.

Directions

From Minneapolis, head west on I-394 for 9 miles. Continue for 17 miles on U.S. Highway 12 West. Turn right onto County Line Road SE for 1.5 miles. Turn right at Delano Rockford Road for 0.5 mile. Continue on Rebecca Park Trail for another 0.5 mile. Turn right at the park entrance and take an immediate left. Turn right 0.2 mile later into the Lake Rebecca boat landing parking lot.

9 CROSBY LAKE TRAIL
Carver Park Reserve, Victoria

Distance: 4 miles round-trip

Duration: 2-2.5 hours

Elevation Change: 50 feet

Effort: Easy/moderate

Trail: Mowed path, wood chips, boardwalk, packed turf

Users: Hikers, leashed dogs

Season: Year-round; cross-country skiing in winter

Passes/Fees: None

Maps: Maps available at the nature center and on the park website

Contact: Carver Park Reserve, Lowry Nature Center, 7025 Victoria Drive, 763/694-7650, www.threeriversparks.org, 5am-10pm daily

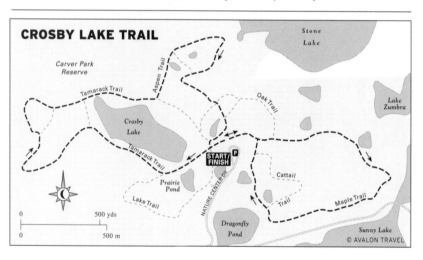

Enjoy extensive boardwalk trails through cattail ponds and tamarack tree marshes.

Peaceful Crosby Lake and its surrounding wetlands and prairie meadows are a world away from the highway.

Start the Hike

From the parking lot, walk behind the **nature center** and take a right on the path bedded with wood chips. The **Lowry Nature Center trail system** is divided into small loops, each named after a tree that dominates the park's wooded areas. This portion of the trail is called **Maple.** Stay left at the first trail intersection, but take a right at the second one 200 feet up the trail.

About 600 feet into the **Maple loop,** an overlook gives you a sweeping view of the wide cattail pond the trail traces. A few feet from the lookout point is a **wooden bridge** that crosses the creek that feeds the pond; 0.25 mile ahead, you will walk several hundred feet along a **boardwalk** among the cattails directly across the pond from the look-

Bluebird houses like this one are helping the Eastern Bluebird thrive near Crosby Lake.

out point. In another 0.25 mile, the **Cattail trail** breaks off to the right. Stay to your left here and once more in another 500 feet where the Cattail trail starts. Take a left at the next intersection. The **Maple trail** makes an approximately 1.5-mile loop and brings you back behind the visitors center.

Keep a steady course here and walk straight through the educational play areas and small gardens surrounding the building. After passing the **butterfly garden** on your left, the trail becomes a mowed grass path through the prairie hills that surround Crosby Lake.

Just beyond **Crosby Rock** (a monument dedicated to the area's late landowner), follow the trail to the right along the ridge above the lake. A narrow mowed path branches to the right 0.25 mile from Crosby Rock. Keep to your left on the main path. Another 0.25 mile through the grassy hills brings you to another intersection. Make a hard right turn onto the **wooded ridgeline trail.** You leave the grassland behind here and enter the oak and maple forest that borders the northern edge of the lake; 500 feet from the intersection, the **Tamarack boardwalk trail** dips down from the wooded ridge into the marsh. Take a left down the hill to the boardwalk.

Most of the land here just north of Crosby Lake and west of Stone Lake is a vast wetland marsh. The Tamarack trail boardwalk puts you right in the heart of it, looping through the silent, swampy stands of dead tamarack trees. After 600 feet of boardwalk, the trail climbs back up the ridge.

At the top of the ridge, take a left and walk 0.25 mile along the northern shore of **Crosby Lake.** At the next intersection, take a left onto the **Aspen trail.** The path leads through—you guessed it—aspen trees. You will cross the third boardwalk of this hike. Use caution when crossing, as the boards can get wet. An overlook 0.25 mile from the end of the boardwalk gives another view of the expansive wetland on the western shore of Stone Lake.

Choose the middle path at the trail intersection 0.1 mile from the overlook point. You are hooking on to part of the **Oak trail** here on your way back to the trailhead. Take another left a few hundred feet later and then one more. This brings you near the **butterfly garden** at the beginning of the Tamarack trail. The visitors center is in sight, and the trail leads you to your starting point at the trailhead parking lot.

Extend the Hike

To dip back into another wetland area after finishing this hike, take the Lake trail past Prairie Pond after returning to the nature center. The Lake trail leads south from the butterfly garden and adds nearly 1 mile to your hike.

Directions

From Minneapolis, take I-394 West for 9 miles, then turn left onto I-494 South for 3.7 miles. Exit onto MN 7 West for 13.5 miles. Turn left onto Victoria Drive for 1.2 miles and make another left at Nature Center Drive for 1 mile to the Lowry Nature Center parking lot.

10 LUNDSTEN LAKE LOOP

Carver Park Reserve, Victoria

Distance: 4.8 miles round-trip

Duration: 2.5 hours

Elevation Change: Negligible

Effort: Easy/moderate

Trail: Gravel road, dirt, forest turf

Users: Hikers, cyclists, horse riders, leashed dogs

Season: Year-round; cross-country skiing in winter

Passes/Fees: None

Maps: Maps available at the nature center and on the park website

Contact: Carver Park Reserve, Lowry Nature Center, 7025 Victoria Drive, 763/694-7650, www.threeriversparks.org, 5am-10pm daily

---

Hike along the overlooks of Lundsten Lake's rolling prairies and wetlands.

Located in the southwestern corner of Carver Park Reserve, this peaceful hiking trail loops around the lake and is shared with horse riders.

Start the Hike

From the parking lot, walk north along the park road you took to get to the parking area for 0.25 mile. Take a left on the **wide dirt trail** that leads northwest. Follow it for 0.7 mile across the creek that connects to **Lake Auburn** and to the intersection just south of the **paved hiker/cyclist trail.** If you get to the pavement, you have gone too far. A wide dirt trail leads to the west just before the pavement and is easy to find.

The trail passes through a large stand of oak, maple, and basswood trees for 0.5 mile past an overlook point just prior to the next trail intersection. Stay to the left

This chewed-off stump is a sure sign that beaver are close by.

and continue hiking straight west for 0.4 mile to the **group picnic and campsite parking lot.** Stay to the left as the trail swings south and crosses a tree-lined **land bridge** along the western shore of the lake.

After crossing the lake, you pass a cross-country-ski-only trail that veers to the left. Keep to your right and follow the trail south for 0.7 mile along the farmland and **Parley Lake Road** to the west. The trail curves east and borders Highway 5 for 1.25 miles. When the trail curves north, it will lead 0.5 mile back to the park road. Take a left and complete the remaining 0.25 mile back to the parking lot.

Hike Nearby

Just before the first trail intersection with the paved bike trail, the hiking path branches to the right for 1.25 miles around Lake 2. Take this route to add the extra distance and pass through a more wooded area of oak and maple forest. Stay left at the two unpaved hiking trail intersections and take a right at the third to head west on the main hiking trail.

Directions

From Minneapolis, take I-394 West for 9 miles; then turn left onto I-494 South for 3.7 miles. Exit onto MN 7 West for 13.5 miles. Turn left onto Victoria Drive for 1.2 miles and then right at Carver Park Road for 1 mile to the King Blind parking lot.

11 MINNETONKA TRAIL

Lake Minnetonka Regional Park, Minnetrista

Distance: 1 mile round-trip

Duration: 0.5-1 hour

Elevation Change: Negligible

Effort: Easy

Trail: Paved, gravel road

Users: Hikers, cyclists, leashed dogs

Season: Year-round; snowshoeing in winter

Passes/Fees: $5 daily vehicle permit fee

Maps: Maps available at the visitors center and on the park website

Contact: Lake Minnetonka Regional Park, 4610 County Road 44, 763/694-7754, www.threeriversparks.org, 6am-sunset daily

---

This creek-side trail is a quick and peaceful escape from the hubbub of the city.

Lake Minnetonka Regional Park is a pleasant place to stretch your legs and get a little nature time in.

Start the Hike

The hiking trail begins at the small parking area. For the first 0.13 mile, the path runs parallel to a paved hiker/cyclist trail until crossing under the **County Road 44 bridge;** 0.25 mile from the parking lot, the wide gravel trail transitions into a narrow **forest turf path** under a canopy of oak and maple trees.

A winding creek bed crisscrosses the path several times here. At some points, you may need to rock hop if the water is high.

The far end of this trail makes a 0.2-mile loop through the shady forest landscape.

At the end of the loop, walk back toward the parking lot and out of the woods. The waist-high grasses near the trailhead usher you back to the trailhead and parking lot.

© JAKE KULJU

This shady canopy of maple leaves is a great way to beat the heat at Lake Minnetonka.

Extend the Hike

If you'd like to get a view of the park's namesake lake, cross the road after returning to the parking lot and follow the paved hiker/cyclist path to your left. After curving clockwise for 0.25 mile past the picnic area and into a large parking lot, take another left onto an unpaved hiking trail. This path leads to the boat landing on the shore of Lake Minnetonka and is a great way to add 0.5 mile to this short hike. This route can turn into an extremely family-friendly hike. The path leads through two picnic areas and a playground with slides, swings, and sandboxes.

Directions

From Minneapolis, take I-394 West for 9 miles; then turn left onto I-494 South for 3.7 miles. Exit onto MN 7 West for 12 miles. Turn right on County Road 44 for 0.2 mile and then make another right into the park entrance. Drive past the entry station and turn left. The hiking/dog trail parking lot is 0.1 mile ahead on your left.

12 CROW RIVER LOOP
Crow-Hassan Park Reserve, Hanover

Best: Wildflowers

Distance: 5.7 miles round-trip

Duration: 3 hours

Elevation Change: 50 feet

Effort: Moderate

Trail: Packed turf

Users: Hikers, leashed dogs

Season: April-October; cross-country skiing and snowshoeing in winter

Passes/Fees: None

Maps: Maps available on the park website

Contact: Crow-Hassan Park Reserve, 12595 Park Drive, Hanover, 763/694-7860, www.threeriversparks.org, 5am-10pm daily

---

Hike along the high banks of the Crow River.

For a real prairie experience, there's no place like Crow-Hassan Park near St. Michael. This grassy nook in a bend of the Crow River is a paradise of rolling hills, grassy expanses, and colorful prairie flowers.

Start the Hike
Take the trail that heads north from the parking lot, staying to your right at the two intersections in the first 0.25 mile. The next 1.5 miles pass through open prairie.

At the third trail intersection, take a left as the path threads between **North and South Twin Lakes.** The trail breaks into three prongs 0.25 mile ahead. Take the **rightmost path.** This stretch leads slightly upward, and the vastness of the

© JAKE KULJU

White yarrow flowers fill the grassy fields of Crow-Hassan Park Reserve.

prairie landscape is revealed to you on all sides. In another 0.25 mile, the trail again gives you three choices. This time take the **middle road,** which leads farther north. As the trail curves to the left, you enter the forest canopy, primarily made up of elm and maple trees.

As you head west, the trail gets closer to the river; 2.25 miles into the hike, you get a nice view of the **Crow River.** Shortly thereafter, you come upon a cross-country ski trail intersection. Stay to the right (the path to the left is usually overgrown with grass in summer, anyway). Here the trail cuts away from the riverbank and makes a more dramatic turn to the south. After passing through a small marshland, the trail briefly arcs westward and then straightens out toward the **Bluestem Group Camp area** at the 3.5-mile mark. You'll know you're there when you see the large abandoned barn. Another view of the river awaits you after crossing the access road. In a few hundred feet you come upon **Crow River Group Camp.** Cross this camp's access road and you soon come upon **wooden stairs** that lead to the canoe access site at the water's edge.

When the trail turns to your left, you will soon break out of the woods and return to the prairie. At the next trail intersection take a right, continuing to follow the river. In another 0.25 mile take two left turns, about 50 feet from each other, to point you in the direction of the parking lot. This last 0.5-mile stretch is alternating grassland and forest.

Extend the Hike
To get more time along the river and to tack another 2 miles onto this hike,

continue straight at the final turn, making a left at the second intersection onto the northward-leading dog/hiking trail. The trail meets the road near the park entrance. Take a left here back to the parking lot.

Directions

From Minneapolis, take I-94 West for 22 miles. Take the Rogers exit and turn left onto Main Street for 0.5 mile. Turn right at 129th Avenue for 1.8 miles and then turn right at Territorial Road for 0.5 mile. Turn left onto Hassan Parkway for 1.4 miles. Turn right at Ghostley Road for 0.5 mile. Drive past the entry station and park in the Trailhead parking lot.

13 LAKE KATRINA LOOP
Baker Park Reserve, Maple Plain

Distance: 5.5 miles round-trip

Duration: 2.5-3 hours

Elevation Change: Negligible

Effort: Easy/moderate

Trail: Packed turf

Users: Hikers, cyclists

Season: Year-round; cross-country skiing in winter

Passes/Fees: None

Maps: Maps available at the trailhead and on the park website

Contact: Baker Park Reserve, 2301 County Road 19, 763/694-7662, www. threeriversparks.org, 5am-10pm daily

---

Walk around secluded Lake Katrina in Baker Park Reserve.

The serene, wide, grassy forest turf trail that loops around Lake Katrina is a hiker's paradise.

Start the Hike
From the parking lot, both the unpaved and paved hiking paths are visible. Take a right on the **unpaved path** and begin the **counterclockwise loop** around the lake. The first 0.25 mile will be through light forest cover, but the trail soon enters an open tallgrass prairie landscape

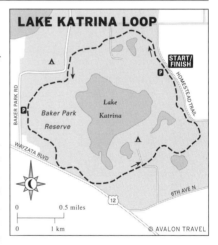

with scattered trees and shrubs. From this slightly elevated area above the lake, you can watch how the lake transitions to marsh, then sedge, prairie, and forest.

At 1.3 miles, you will come to a trail intersection at **Oak Knoll Group Camp.** Stay to your left and cross two paved hiker/cyclist paths about 100 feet from each other. The next mile takes you near **three small ponds** in the wetland system that borders the lake. As the trail swings back south after these ponds, you enter

© JAKE KULJU

Plumes of tallgrass sway in the breeze along Lake Katrina's grassy sides.

another wooded area. At the **3-mile point,** you will be near Highway 12 and the large cattail field on the southern shore of the lake.

The trail borders Highway 12 for a few hundred feet, then breaks northeast. Four miles in, you'll cross the road to the **Katrina Group Camp.** The trail continues eastward, entering more rolling prairie grassland. Stay left at the upcoming trail intersection where the path turns northward. This marks the last 0.75 mile to the trailhead. A wildlife management area lies to your left. From here you pass through one more patch of trees before reaching the parking lot.

Extend the Hike

To visit the beach at Lake Independence, take a right after the Oak Knoll Group Camp onto the paved hiker/cyclist trail. This trail leads to the camping area and lakeside recreation area on Lake Independence and puts an extra 0.5 mile on your hike. It is also a more family-friendly option.

Directions

From Minneapolis, drive west on I-394 for 9 miles. Continue on U.S. Highway 12 West for 7.7 miles. Turn right at Old Crystal Bay Road for 0.5 mile. Turn left at 6th Avenue N for 0.2 mile and then right for 1.5 miles on Homestead Trail. The Horse/Hike/Bike Trail parking lot is on your left.

14 LAKE MINNEWASHTA AND WOODLAND LOOP TRAILS

Lake Minnewashta Regional Park, Chanhassen

Distance: 2.65 miles round-trip

Duration: 2 hours

Elevation Change: 30 feet

Effort: Easy

Trail: Packed turf, dirt

Users: Hikers, leashed dogs

Season: Year-round

Passes/Fees: $5 daily vehicle permit fee

Maps: Maps available at the park entrance and on the park website

Contact: Lake Minnewashta Regional Park, 6900 Hazeltine Boulevard, Chanhassen, 952/466-5250, www.co.carver.mn.us, 6am-10pm daily

---

Follow the shores of Lake Minnewashta in Lake Minnewashta Regional Park.

The Lake and Woodland Loop Trails will take you from marshy shores to breezy fields.

Start the Hike

From the beach parking lot, walk to your left near the vending machines. The **Lake Trail** begins here and wraps north around the peninsula that juts into Lake Minnewashta. Take a right past the beach and the restroom facility and walk along the northern edge of the parking lot through the maple trees. This low trail can be wet and muddy in spring and after heavy rains. A half mile from the trailhead, the Lake Trail nears the small, marshy bay the park encompasses. The trail turns south here and leads to the **boat landing.**

You come to a small parking lot and **picnic area** 1.25 miles into the hike. Take a right when the trail splits and begin walking **counterclockwise** along the **Woodland Loop Trail.** The path climbs slightly to a more open area with scattered trees and fields. This loop is 1.4 miles long and has two cross trails within it. **Stay to the right at each intersection** to remain on the Woodland Loop Trail. Returning south on the loop trail, you reenter the wooded area that hugs the lakeshore. When you return to the picnic area, pick up the Lake Trail and head back through the trees to the parking lot.

A willow tree arcs over the water in Lake Minnewashta Regional Park.

Extend the Hike

To get a taste of more of the park's lowlands, head down the Cattail Trail leading south from the beach parking lot. The path connects with the Prairie Loop trail and adds 1.5 miles to your hike.

Directions

From Minneapolis, take I-394 West for 9 miles; then turn left onto I-494 South for 3.7 miles. Exit onto MN 7 West for 7 miles. Turn left at MN 41 North. The park entrance is in 1 mile on your right. Follow signs to the beach parking lot.

15 FISH LAKE TRAIL

Fish Lake Regional Park, Maple Grove

Distance: 2.6 miles round-trip

Duration: 1.5 hours

Elevation Change: 30 feet

Effort: Easy

Trail: Paved, mowed path, gravel road, packed turf

Users: Hikers, cyclists, leashed dogs

Season: Year-round; snowshoeing in winter

Passes/Fees: None

Maps: Maps available on the park website

Contact: Fish Lake Regional Park, 14900 Bass Lake Road, 763/694-7818, www.threeriversparks.org, 5am-10pm daily

---

Explore the southern inlet and wooded peninsula of Fish Lake.

Fish Lake is a favorite of anglers and has an excellent trail system.

Start the Hike

Begin by climbing the hill north of the pavilion. A short **service road** goes to the top, and a **mowed grass path** continues for another 200 feet. A small clearing with a fire ring sits atop the hill. At the northern edge of the hill, a small **footpath** leads down to the water. Take a left on the **paved hiker/ cyclist trail** and arc past the beach to the parking area. Follow the paved hiker/cyclist path along the edge of the parking lot and then turn left, crossing the park road. An **unpaved path** joins the trail here.

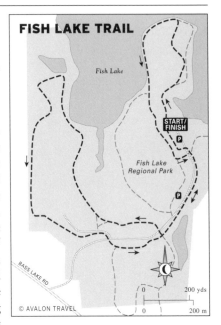

Take a right onto the unpaved path and follow it alongside the road for about 0.1 mile; 0.3 mile into the hike, you will come to another **paved hiker/cyclist path.** Take a right on it and follow the path for 0.1 mile as it crosses the **park road** and heads west. After crossing the **bridge** built over the creek, veer right on the **unpaved path.** You will be heading north toward the lake on the west side of the inlet. This forest turf trail arcs for nearly a mile through the forest.

At 1.6 miles, you meet another **paved trail.** Take a left on it for 0.2 mile to the maintenance facility road. Take a right to the **park road** just a few hundred feet away. Cross the road and veer left on the **unpaved hiking trail.** This leads you to a **paved trail** intersection 0.1 mile ahead. Cross the intersection and you will find yourself on the path you took earlier alongside the park road. Follow it back to the parking lot 0.25 mile away.

Hike Nearby

To get a more woodsy experience and add another 0.5 mile onto your hike, follow the maintenance facility road south. After reaching the main road, take a short left and an unpaved hiking trail leads into the trees. After curving through the woods for 0.4 mile, take a left on the paved hiker/cyclist trail that leads back to the main road. Take a right here toward the parking lot.

Directions

From Minneapolis, take I-94 West for 13.5 miles. Exit left onto I-494 South for 1.7 miles. Take the County Road 10 exit and turn right onto County Road 10 West for 1.3 miles. Turn right at Fish Lake Park Road. Drive past the entry station and follow the park road to the second parking lot by the picnic area.

MEDICINE LAKE TRAIL
Clifton E. French Regional Park, Plymouth

Distance: 1.5 miles round-trip

Duration: 1 hour

Elevation Change: 40 feet

Effort: Easy

Trail: Sidewalk, packed turf

Users: Hikers, leashed dogs

Season: Year-round

Passes/Fees: None

Maps: Maps available at the visitors center and on the park website

Contact: Clifton E. French Regional Park, 12605 County Road 9, 763/694-7750, www.threeriversparks.org, 5am-10pm daily

---

Follow the winding inlet on the northern end of Medicine Lake.

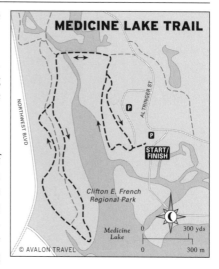

Just west of Minneapolis, Clifton E. French Regional Park is situated along the winding inlet into Medicine Lake that is home to a plethora of wildlife.

Start the Hike
A large set of steps on the right side of the **visitors center** starts you off on this easy hike. Climb the concrete steps and follow the handrail-lined **sidewalk** to the top of the hill behind the building. At the **trail intersection,** follow the middle of the three paths, heading downhill toward the lakeshore. The trail curves to the right and follows the reedy wetland area that surrounds the Medicine Lake inlet. At the **0.3-mile mark,** turn left and walk across the inlet to the other side of the water.

Turn left at the **bench** after crossing the water and climb the small, sandy hill that rises above the lakeshore. Stay to your left at all trail intersections for the

The leaves of the sumac trees on Medicine Lake turn a deep burgundy in mid-autumn.

next 0.5 mile until the trail makes a sharp right turn. Keep left 300 feet later as the trail traces the edge of a wetland area and pond. Just under 0.5 mile from the intersection, choose the middle path, which takes you to the foot of the sandy hill you climbed earlier. Veer left back to the bench and take a right to cross the inlet on your way back to the visitors center.

Extend the Hike

Before crossing the inlet on your way back to the visitors center, keep walking straight on the west side of the water. Cross the footbridge and loop counter-clockwise around the pond and wetland area at the upper part of the inlet. The trail passes by the park's operations center and near Highway 61. This loop will add 0.75 mile to your hike and give you some more time in the quiet trees that surround this peaceful inlet.

Directions

From Minneapolis take I-394 West for 9.2 miles. Exit left onto I-494 North for 4.1 miles. Exit onto County Road 9 and take a right for 0.6 mile. Turn right into the park entrance and follow signs to the visitors center parking lot.

17 ELM CREEK TRAIL

Elm Creek Park Reserve, Maple Grove

Distance: 4.75 miles round-trip

Duration: 3 hours

Elevation Change: Negligible

Effort: Easy/moderate

Trail: Packed turf, boardwalk

Users: Hikers, cyclists

Season: Year-round; snowshoeing in winter

Passes/Fees: None

Maps: Maps available at the nature center and on the park website

Contact: Elm Creek Park Reserve, Eastman Nature Center, 13351 Elm Creek Road, Dayton, 763/694-7700, www.threeriversparks.org, 5am-10pm daily

This hike features rustic footbridges and boardwalks.

The Eastman Nature Center in Elm Creek Park Reserve provides a serene hike through the woods.

Start the Hike

The trail starts across the parking lot from the **nature center,** branching off the road that leads to the nature center. Walk 100 feet on the sidewalk that borders the road and take a left onto the **unpaved hiking trail** that leads northwest. You are walking into a marshy area surrounding a small pond and will eventually walk right through it all on a boardwalk. Make the slight descent to the 307-foot-long **boardwalk** amid the bulrushes, reeds, and lily pads. Be careful if the boardwalk is wet; it can be slippery. Do not jump or stomp on the boardwalk, as the excess motion can disturb the plant life in the pond and soak the boardwalk with marsh water.

The trail makes a sharp left turn on the other end of the pond and heads south to the Sumac Trail. Turn right here toward the **Meadowlark Trail,** named after the grassland bird. This **1.5-mile loop** starts about 0.5 mile into the hike and circles an open grassland on the western edge of the trail system. As the trail turns south, a spur trail leads to a group campsite. Stay to the left and continue on the

Sedge grass grows on the banks of Rush Creek in Elm Creek Park Reserve.

© JAKE KULJU

Meadowlark Trail. When you return to the beginning of the loop, continue ahead and keep right where the **Sumac Trail** enters. Take another right at the next intersection. You have entered the **Oxbow Loop** and will cross a series of five **wooden footbridges** built over the various waterways near Rush Creek. At the bottom of the loop, take a right toward the **Monarch Trail.** On the way, you'll walk out of the trees and follow the edge of the forest adjacent to the rolling grasslands that dominate the second half of this hike.

After taking a right onto the Monarch Trail, you dip in and out of stands of maple trees on your way to **Elm Creek.** Stay to your right at the next trail intersection and cross the **paved hiker/cyclist trail** near the 3.25-mile point. A few hundred feet ahead, you will cross another **unpaved trail** and begin on the **Creek Trail,** which borders Elm Creek. A half mile from the last intersection, take a left and arc across the prairie grasslands north of the creek. After turning south, take a right at the trail intersection and cross the paved hiker/cyclist path to start on the Monarch Trail. The nature center lies 0.25 mile ahead.

Hike Nearby

Instead of taking a left at the end of Creek Trail, take a right and follow the bridge across the creek. This path loops to the right and connects to part of a horse trail. Take a right at all intersections until you reach the paved hiker/cyclist trail. Turn right here and cross the creek until the unpaved path leads slightly to the right. Take a left at the second unpaved intersection after leaving the pavement and you will be on the Monarch Trail and the last leg of the hike.

Directions

From Minneapolis, take I-94 West for 9.7 miles. Exit onto County Road 81 for 6.6 miles. Turn right at Fernbrook Lane North for 1 mile. Take a right at Elm Creek Road for 0.5 mile. A sign to the park entrance will be on your right. Follow this road to the Eastman Nature Center parking lot 0.3 mile from the park entrance.

18 RUM RIVER TRAIL

Rum River Central Regional Park, Ramsey

Distance: 3.25 miles round-trip

Duration: 1.5 hours

Elevation Change: 50 feet

Effort: Easy

Trail: Paved, packed turf

Users: Hikers, cyclists, horse riders, leashed dogs

Season: Year-round

Passes/Fees: $5 daily vehicle permit fee

Maps: Maps available on the park website

Contact: Rum River Central Regional Park, 17955 Roanoke Street NW, 763/767-2820, www.anokacounty.us, 6am-sunset daily

---

Wind through the thick forests along the Rum River.

Rum River Central Regional Park is tucked into the curviest portion of this winding river, where the channel makes several oxbows and dramatically changes direction from southeast to northwest.

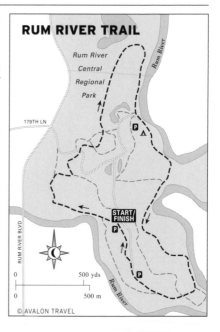

Start the Hike

The **unpaved hiking trail** starts on the northern end of the parking lot and leads west. Take a left onto the path until the trail splits after a few hundred feet. Veer to the right and walk the 0.4-mile arm of trail, keeping to the right through the bottomland forest at the next trail intersection. Take a left at the following junction and head through 0.25 mile of tangled trail crossings, always staying on the wide, **unpaved hiking/horse trail.** At the last crossing of the pavement, the trail moves straight north through thick cottonwood, bass-wood, and maple forest. This 0.6-mile arc follows the river south and meets the paved **hiker/cyclist trail** near the northern parking lot and boat access site. Take a left onto the pavement and continue to follow the south-flowing river for 0.5 mile to the **fishing pier.** There is not much variation in the vegetation in this park.

Continue on the **paved path** as it follows the river south. The path heads southeast into the narrow pinch of land in the river's tightest oxbow, where it crosses the **forest turf trail.** Take a left at this intersection and follow the path further into the forest as it arcs to the northwest past the playground and picnic shelter. The **canoe launch site** lies 0.25 mile ahead. Take a right onto the paved path and walk slightly uphill to the Carry-in Canoe Launch parking lot.

A dry stream bed in the Rum River Valley.

At 0.1 mile after you turn right, sidestep to the **unpaved trail** that parallels the pavement on your left. This trail continues north, following the river during its northward curve, and leads you back to the parking lot.

Shorten the Hike

To shorten this hike by a third and still get to the most scenic parts of the river, take a right when the paved path makes a Y after the fishing pier. At just over a mile, this trail leads through the forest back to the parking lot just under 0.1 mile away.

Directions

From Minneapolis, take I-94 West for 5.3 miles. Exit onto MN 252 North for 3.8 miles. Merge onto MN 610 East for 3 miles; then exit onto MN 47 North for 1 mile. Merge onto U.S. Highway 10 West for 6.5 miles and take the County Road 7 exit. Turn right onto County Road 7 for 6.8 miles. Turn right at the sign for the park entrance. Drive past the gatehouse and take a right turn, following signs to the Carry-in Canoe Launch parking lot.

19 COON RAPIDS DAM TRAIL

Coon Rapids Dam Regional Park, Coon Rapids

Distance: 2.7 miles round-trip

Duration: 1-1.5 hours

Elevation Change: Negligible

Effort: Easy

Trail: Paved, packed turf, dirt

Users: Hikers, leashed dogs

Season: Year-round

Passes/Fees: $5 daily vehicle permit fee

Maps: Maps available at the visitors center and on the park website

Contact: Coon Rapids Dam Regional Park, 9750 Egret Boulevard, Coon Rapids, 763/767-2820, www.anokacounty.us, 6am-sunset daily

---

Cross the Mississippi River over the impressive Coon Rapids Dam.

Just 12 miles upstream from Minneapolis, this park is a unique way to view the Mississippi and a great way to get your feet on the trail.

Start the Hike

Begin at the visitors center and take a left toward the river and the dam. A **paved sidewalk** leads to the structure, and this portion of the hike is wheelchair accessible. Five floodgates surge with overflow water from the reservoir the dam contains. The first section of the dam is a short jaunt to tiny **Dunn Island.** The second stretch is about 0.25-mile long. Huge arcs of river water tumble through the dam's five chutes, creating a roaring, mist-filled experience.

When you reach the west side of the river, take a left and follow the **packed dirt path** that leads away from the pavement. You almost immediately come upon an open **picnic area** with restrooms; 200 feet ahead of this area and to your left is a narrower **turf trail** that holds tightly to the water's edge. The shady cottonwood and basswood trees that overhang the banks of the river are fun for climbing on and around. Anglers frequent this area below the dam and cast their spinners from the large tree roots that dangle into the water. For the next 0.5 mile, enjoy scrambling along the riverside.

When you encounter a larger stream, the downstream portion of the hike is over. Follow the path to the right and cross the **footbridge** 500 feet ahead. Take

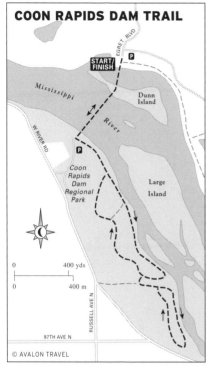

COON RAPIDS DAM TRAIL

an immediate left and follow the **turf trail** through a wooded area near the lower islands of the park. The 0.5-mile loop takes you back to the **footbridge** you previously crossed. Take a left and follow the trail along an open meadow full of waist-high sweetgrass and wild daisies. A quarter mile from the bridge, a **mowed path** leads to your right. Stay to your left and follow the trail back to the picnic and restroom area. From here, cross back over the dam to the visitors center.

Extend the Hike

To add another mile to your hike, you can follow some of the paved hiking and biking trails that lead along the river's east bank. After crossing the dam on your way back to the parking lot, take a right and follow the path to Cenaiko Lake.

Directions

From Minneapolis, take I-94 West for 5.3 miles. Exit onto MN 610 East for 1.6 miles. Take the County Road 1 exit and turn left onto East River Road NW for 1 mile. Veer right onto Coon Rapids Boulevard NW for 0.7 mile. Turn left at Egret Boulevard NW for 0.5 mile. Drive past the entry station and park at the Anoka Visitor Center parking lot.

ST. CROIX RIVER VALLEY

© JAKE KULJU

The St. Croix River is known for its rocky and cliff-lined shores with hard basalt and sandstone formations. Rapids and waterfalls are common, drawing kayakers and canoeists to its white water, and its surrounding shores and bluffs make for great hiking. The Mississippi, St. Croix, and Vermillion Rivers meet in the city of Hastings, and the Mississippi River carries these waters south into true bluff country. Across the border in Wisconsin, trails climb the undulating bluffs that rise helter-skelter from the ground. The rapid-filled St. Louis River feeds Lake Superior, and the Grand Portage Trail along the St. Louis is the same centuries-old voyageur portaging trail that French trappers and explorers used in the 1700s. Hikes along the Vermillion, Kinnickinnic, and Whitewater Rivers take you through the thick forests that surround tributaries to the St. Croix.

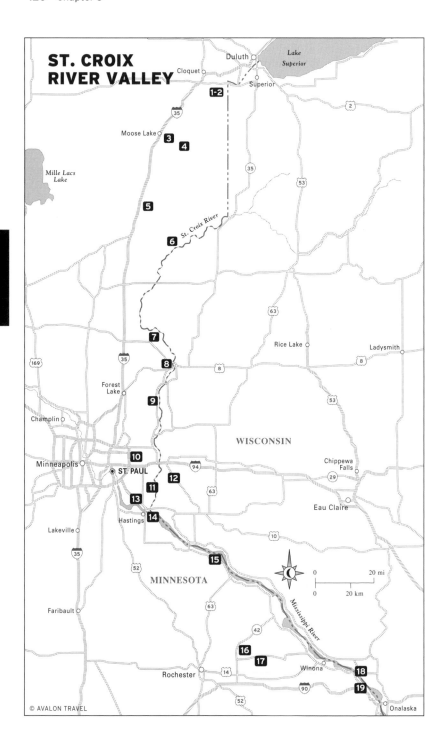

ST. CROIX
RIVER VALLEY

TRAIL NAME	LEVEL	DISTANCE	TIME	ELEVATION	PAGE
1 Grand Portage Trail	Moderate/strenuous	4.2 mi rt	2.5 hr	360 ft	122
2 Swinging Bridge and Summer Trail Loop	Moderate	3.75 mi rt	2 hr	180 ft	125
3 Rolling Hills and Echo Lake Trail	Moderate	4.7 mi rt	2.5 hr	200 ft	128
4 Christmas Tree Trail	Easy	2 mi rt	1-1.5 hr	30 ft	130
5 Quarry Loop to High Bluff Trail	Moderate	3 mi rt	1.5 hr	200 ft	132
6 Kettle River and Bear Creek Trail	Moderate	6.2 mi rt	3.5-4 hr	30 ft	135
7 Deer Creek Loop and River Trail	Moderate	7.3 mi rt	4 hr	120 ft	137
8 River Trail to Sandstone Bluffs	Moderate/strenuous	3.75 mi rt	2.5-3 hr	250 ft	139
9 Prairie Overlook and Woodland Edge Loop	Moderate	5.7 mi rt	2.5-3 hr	160 ft	142
10 Eagle Point Lake Trail	Easy/moderate	4.5 mi rt	2.5-3 hr	Negligible	145
11 St. Croix River Trail	Moderate	4 mi rt	2-2.5 hr	180 ft	147
12 Kinni Canyon Trail	Moderate	3.7 mi rt	2.5-3 hr	60 ft	149
13 Cottage Grove Ravine Trails	Moderate	2.8 mi rt	2.5 hr	150 ft	151
14 Vermillion Falls Trail	Easy/moderate	4.6 mi rt	2.5 hr	Negligible	153
15 Lake Pepin Overlook Hiking Club Trail	Moderate	3.3 mi rt	2 hr	220 ft	155
16 Riverbend Trail	Moderate/strenuous	3.1 mi rt	2 hr	350 ft	157
17 Dakota and Trout Run Creek Trails	Strenuous	6.7 mi rt	4.5 hr	400 ft	159
18 Riverview Trail to Blufftop Trail	Strenuous	4.5 mi rt	3 hr	420 ft	162
19 King's and Queen's Bluff Trail	Moderate	4.5 mi rt	2.5-3 hr	220 ft	165

1 GRAND PORTAGE TRAIL

Jay Cooke State Park, Carlton

Best: Historical Hikes

Distance: 4.2 miles round-trip

Duration: 2.5 hours

Elevation Change: 360 feet

Effort: Moderate/strenuous

Trail: Packed turf

Users: Hikers, leashed dogs

Season: April-October

Passes/Fees: $5 daily vehicle permit fee

Maps: Maps available at the park office and on the park website

Contact: Jay Cooke State Park, 780 MN 210, 218/384-4610, www.dnr.state.mn.us, 8am-10pm daily

---

Walk along a centuries-old path once frequented by the hardy voyageurs and Native Americans.

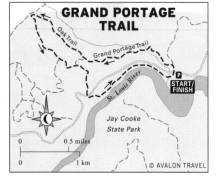

At Jay Cooke State Park, you can actually walk along the historic path that the voyageurs took along the St. Louis River.

Start the Hike

The trailhead is to the left of the parking lot toward the train tracks. An **information kiosk** gives some history of the trail area and displays a likeness of a 1700s voyageur. From the kiosk, take a left onto the trail as it enters the underbrush of the forest. (The first few hundred feet are also the beginning of the famous Superior Hiking Trail.) If you'd like to set foot on the bank of the **St. Louis River** where the original portage began, take a right and you'll get to the water in about 100 feet.

The trail almost immediately crosses the **paved park road** and dives back into the woods. A quarter mile later, the trail dips down to a **small creek.** The water level is usually quite low, and you can rock-hop across. From here you begin a

© JAKE KULJU

the St. Louis River

150-foot ascent over 0.75 mile. While most of this hike is in the thick forest, this is the thickest of it.

One mile into the hike, at the top of the hill, you come to a **wooden marker** with the number **24** emblazoned on it. Take a right here onto the **Oak Trail.** This trail is a loop that follows the top of the ridge and has somewhat of an oak savanna, though no naturalist would call it that. Oak trees do dominate the forest here, though. The **wooden 22 marker** is the 2.5-mile mark from the trailhead. Take a right here and begin a steep descent toward **Gill Creek.** This 0.5-mile portion of the trail descends 140 feet. Cross the park road at **wooden marker 23** and walk to your left to where the trail picks up again. The scenery opens up a bit here as the trail approaches the river.

From the park road along the river to the trailhead is the final mile of the hike. The trail bounces along the riverbank, coming right up to the water and easing back into the trees several times before hugging the park road in the final 0.1 mile to the parking lot. This flat stretch along the river is a nice way to finish the ups and downs of this challenging northwoods hike.

Extend the Hike

If you'd like to add a panoramic view to this outing, you'll have to tack on a few miles, but it's worth it. Take a right at wooden marker 21 and follow the trail as it descends to Gill Creek and then climbs 150 feet to marker 19. Take a left here and another left onto the wider horse/hiking trail at marker 18; a 0.5-mile walk from here will lead you to a trail shelter and a lookout point over the St. Louis River as it flows northwest. Head back the way you came and take a right at marker 21 to rejoin the main hiking trail. This addition will put 2.1 more miles under your belt!

Directions

From St. Paul, head north on I-35 East/I-35 for 128 miles. Exit right onto MN 210 for 7 miles. Drive 3 miles past the park entrance to the Grand Portage Trail parking area on the right.

2 SWINGING BRIDGE AND SUMMER TRAIL LOOP

Jay Cooke State Park, Carlton

Best: River Hikes, Viewing Wildlife

Distance: 3.75 miles round-trip

Duration: 2 hours

Elevation Change: 180 feet

Effort: Moderate

Trail: Packed turf, stone

Users: Hikers, leashed dogs

Season: April-October

Passes/Fees: $5 daily vehicle permit fee

Maps: Maps available at the park office and on the park website

Contact: Jay Cooke State Park, 780 MN 210, 218/384-4610, www.dnr.state. mn.us, 8am-10pm daily

Cross the swinging footbridge over the boulder-laden St. Louis River and walk through the thick forests that surround Silver Creek.

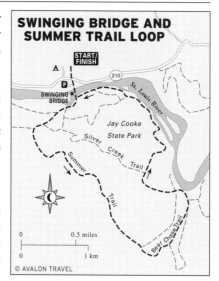

This rocky hike is an adventure and a geology lesson all wrapped into one. Large upturned slate beds jut from the earth where the swiftly moving waters have exposed them.

Start the Hike

From the parking lot, walk to the left of the visitors center and down toward the river. A sign points to the **swinging suspension bridge,** which is where this hike starts.

The first 200 feet of the hike is on this suspension bridge over the tumultuous St. Louis River. Once you are across

Upturned sheets of slate and greywacke line the St. Louis River rapids.

the bridge, stay to your right near the water as the trail moves toward a larger pool along a branch of the river off of the main channel. Veer left here onto the trail that enters the woods. As you move away from the water, you will come upon **three trail intersections.** Turn left at the third onto the wide, grassy path through the forest. This is **Summer Trail,** 0.5 mile from the trailhead. It leads away from the water, south into the forest.

A gentle decline through the forest leads you to **Silver Creek.** Cross the little stream and continue south through the thick maple and basswood trees. You will almost certainly see a few whitetail deer in this secluded area. Bears can be around as well, though they are rarely sighted. At 0.2 mile from the creek, the trail crosses the smaller south branch of Silver Creek and begins a 50-foot ascent at the **Silver Creek backpacking campsite** on your left. The trail turns east here, arcing back toward the river.

Half a mile from the campsite, take a right at the trail intersection onto the **Bear Chase Trail.** Take three lefts over the next 0.5 mile to a quaint wooden **trail shelter** that sits on a high bank overlooking a sharp turn of the river. The trail cuts west here for a few hundred feet and then meets an intersection. Keep straight ahead and take a right at the next intersection 0.25 mile away. You'll pass another **wooden shelter** on your right before the path begins running adjacent to the river.

A gradual 60-foot incline greets you along this river walk during the final 0.75 mile; 0.25 mile from the swinging bridge, you reenter the craggy, angled rock formations. Pick your way along the trail to the bridge and enjoy the cascading water, the sound of the rapids, and the breeze that usually blows here above the river.

Shorten the Hike

To stay close to the St. Louis River on this hike, follow the rocky Carlton Trail, which skims the river's shore. Take a right after crossing the footbridge; hike to marker 27 and back for a 2.5-mile trip.

Directions

From St. Paul, head north on I-35 East/I-35 for 128 miles. Exit right onto MN 210 for 7 miles. Take a right into the park entrance and visitors center parking lot.

3 ROLLING HILLS AND ECHO LAKE TRAIL

Moose Lake State Park, Moose Lake

Distance: 4.7 miles round-trip

Duration: 2.5 hours

Elevation Change: 200 feet

Effort: Moderate

Trail: Mowed grass, packed turf

Users: Hikers, leashed dogs

Season: April-October; snowshoeing in winter

Passes/Fees: $5 daily vehicle permit fee

Maps: Maps available at the park office and on the park website

Contact: Moose Lake State Park, 4252 County Road 137, 218/485-5420, www. dnr.state.mn.us, 8am-10pm daily

Circle through the pine forest near Echo Lake.

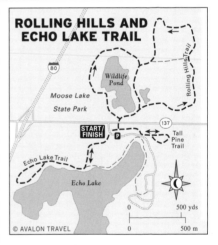

This trail will take you through some of the most beautiful northwoods landscape in the region.

Start the Hike

Head east from the parking lot and follow the blue **Hiking Club trail signs** to your left at the first trail intersection just a few hundred feet from the parking lot. The grass and gravel trail crosses a park road in another hundred feet and then splits. Take a right, following the Hiking Club trail signs. This 0.1-mile trail section crosses a grassy dam on the south shore of **Wildlife Pond.** Take a right after crossing the dam to enter the **Rolling Hills Trail loop.** The path is a wide mowed grass trail lined with thick forest.

In 1.2 miles, the path arcs through dense forest and several hills, climbing 140 feet uphill. When you reach the **wooden shelter,** remain left on the wider path that borders the western shore of Wildlife Pond; 0.2 mile from the shelter, take a right onto the narrower path that loops around the entire body of water.

When you return to the **trail intersection** near the wooden shelter, take a right onto the grassy path and another right 0.2 mile later to **cross the dam.** Take a left, leaving the Hiking Club trail and crossing the **park road** toward the trailhead. Take a left at the intersection after the road onto the **Tall Pine Trail.** This spur loop leads through tall, majestic red pines. The 0.3-mile loop takes you up and down both sides of the small hill the pine grove is on and then returns you to the trailhead. Take a left at the parking lot and follow the road to the beach parking lot for 0.2 mile.

Peaceful pines sway in the breeze along the Tall Pine Trail.

The final 1.2 miles follow a section of the northern shore of beautiful **Echo Lake.** Take a right at the sandy beach and walk past a shaded picnic area; then climb a small hill along the **Echo Lake Trail loop.** When you return to the beach, walk back north through the parking lot along the park road to the trailhead.

Extend the Hike

For another 0.5 mile and more time along the lakeshore, keep along the water's edge when you return to the Echo Lake beach. This path winds south to the campground. Turn around at the park road and follow the path back to the beach. Then take a right and head north to the parking lot.

Directions

From St. Paul, head north on I-35 East/I-35 for 107 miles. Exit onto MN 73 toward Moose Lake for 0.3 mile. Turn right at County Road 137 for 0.4 mile, crossing over the freeway. Turn right into the park entrance in 0.1 mile. Park in the lot just across from the park office.

❹ CHRISTMAS TREE TRAIL

Nemadji State Forest, Holyoke

Distance: 2 miles round-trip

Duration: 1-1.5 hours

Elevation Change: 30 feet

Effort: Easy

Trail: Mowed grass, packed turf

Users: Hikers, leashed dogs

Season: Year-round; cross-country skiing and snowshoeing in winter

Passes/Fees: None

Maps: Maps available on the park website

Contact: Moose Lake Area Office, 218/485-5410, www.dnr.state.mn.us, 6am-10pm daily

---

Walk through thick stands of Norway pine and secluded wetland habitats along the National Christmas Tree Trail deep in the northwoods.

In 1977, a tree on this trail was cut for the president and displayed at the White House, giving the trail its unique name. The little-used Christmas Tree Trail loops through some of the most pristine northwoods forest in this area of the state. The silence and solemnity of the Nemadji State Forest is as complete as it comes.

Start the Hike

The trailhead begins near a stand of birch trees at the outdoor restroom in the **Gaffert Campground** and heads straight north. A metal gate blocks access to motor vehicles, opening to a wide and grassy path. Mowed only a few times a year, the first 0.5 mile is a wild tangle of underbrush tallgrass that winds through a dense pine forest. When the **trail splits,** veer to the right. After the turn, the trail makes its way east toward **Cranberry Lake;** 0.75 mile into the hike, the wide

© JAKE KULJU

Wild blackberries grow along the Christmas Tree Trail.

trail arcs northward and enters a more open area near the creek that flows into Cranberry Lake.

Not far from the creek, a spur trail on your right heads north to **Net River.** The waterway is about 0.2 mile from the trail loop and marks the halfway point of the hike. This completely undeveloped portion of the forest is an example of what much of Minnesota looked like before settlement. When you return to the trail loop, take a right into the thick pines.

The **next trail intersection** is at the bottom of the loop, 1.6 miles into the hike by the same stand of birch trees that greeted you at the beginning of the hike. Take a right here and follow the trail as it meanders south back to the trailhead.

Extend the Hike

For more immersion in the pine forest, take a right on the campground road that you drove along to the trailhead and take a right on the narrow gravel road that heads north to Net Lake. This tree-lined road leads to the southeast corner of Net Lake and gives you a wider perspective of the pine forests and wetland areas of the park while adding 1.2 miles to your hike.

Directions

From St. Paul, head north on I-35 East/I-35 for 88 miles. Exit right onto MN 23 for 30 miles. Turn right at County Road 8 for 1.1 miles. Veer right to continue on County Road 8 for another 1.7 miles. Turn right at County Road 145 for 0.5 mile. Turn left and stay on County Road 145 for 1.5 miles. The trail parking lot is at the intersection of Harlis Road from the east.

5 QUARRY LOOP TO HIGH BLUFF TRAIL

Banning State Park, Sandstone

Best: River Hike

Distance: 3 miles round-trip

Duration: 1.5 hours

Elevation Change: 200 feet

Effort: Moderate

Trail: Packed turf, rocks, dirt

Users: Hikers, leashed dogs

Season: Year-round; cross-country skiing in winter

Passes/Fees: $5 daily vehicle permit fee

Maps: Maps available at the park office and on the park website

Contact: Banning State Park, 61101 Banning Park Rd., Sandstone, 320/245-2668, www.dnr.state.mn.us, 8am-10pm daily

---

Climb the craggy rock formations along a cascading section of the Kettle River.

The Kettle River tears a rapid-filled ravine through the park, exposing towering sandstone formations and rushing waters below the cliffs.

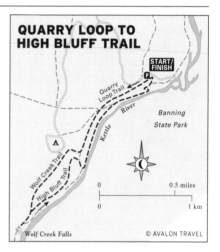

Start the Hike

The **Quarry Loop Trail** leads west from the parking lot. Stone steps take you down close to the cascading Kettle River. Veer right when the trail splits near the trailhead. Stay on the Quarry Loop Trail through three trail intersections.

From the trailhead, after 0.8 mile take a right onto **Deadman Trail** just beyond the old quarry site. The trail here climbs a small hill into thicker deciduous trees. At the top of this 0.1-mile connecting trail, take a left onto the **Wolf Creek Trail;**

© JAKE KULJU

Norway pines take root among the rocks in Banning State Park near the old quarry site.

0.6 mile of trail through thick forest leads away from the river toward **Wolf Creek Falls.** You will see some patches of exposed bedrock along Wolf Creek Trail and pools of water in the rocks after rains and during wet seasons. At the bottom of the falls, the creek makes a wide, deep pool.

Turn around here and walk up from the creek to **High Bluff Trail** at the top of the hill. Veer right into the gnarled red pine trees that grow amid the boulder field. On top of the cliffs that line the river near **Hell's Gate,** you will be 40 feet above the rushing water. Many times the trail seemingly disappears in the layers of rock and blanket of pine needles. Keep your eyes open for the narrow forest turf trail that winds along the craggy bluff for 0.7 mile back to **Deadman Trail.** Take a right here back to **Quarry Loop.** More stone steps take you closer to the river and along the second half of the Quarry Loop. Here you walk through the thickest boulder field, past the old powerhouse and crusher sites from the abandoned quarry works.

Near the end of the loop, take a right to **Teacher's Overlook.** The 0.1-mile spur trail is worth the view over Kettle River. Return to Quarry Loop and take a right. The trailhead is just a few hundred feet from the last intersection.

Extend the Hike

Upstream from the rock formations, the Skunk Cabbage Trail loop follows a more peaceful stretch of the river and takes you deeper into the woods, adding 2.2 miles to your hike. Take a right after returning to the parking lot onto the Skunk Cabbage Trail. After crossing the park road, the trail makes a wide loop through the forest. Follow signs for the Skunk Cabbage Trail at the two intersections until returning to the north side of the parking lot. Cross the park road back to the trailhead to finish the loop.

Directions

From St. Paul, head north on I-35 East/I-35 for 88 miles. Exit right onto MN 23 for 0.4 mile. Turn right at Banning Park Road for 0.1 mile into the park entrance. Drive past the park office and veer left for approximately 1 mile, following signs to the picnic area parking lot.

6 KETTLE RIVER AND BEAR CREEK TRAIL

St. Croix State Park, Hinckley

Distance: 6.2 miles round-trip

Duration: 3.5-4 hours

Elevation Change: 30 feet

Effort: Moderate

Trail: Gravel road, packed turf

Users: Hikers, leashed dogs

Season: Year-round; cross-country skiing in winter

Passes/Fees: $5 daily vehicle permit fee

Maps: Maps available at the park office and on the park website

Contact: St. Croix State Park, 30065 St. Croix Park Rd., Hinckley, 320/384-6591, www.dnr.state.mn.us, 8am-10pm daily

---

Walk to the confluence of the Kettle and St. Croix Rivers.

This expansive park has several trail systems, including one that leads to the confluence of the St. Croix and Kettle Rivers.

Start the Hike

This hike starts out at the parking lot with a beautiful overlook of a sharp bend in the **Kettle River.** Walk back to the gravel road and take a right. Look for the trail to start on your right-hand side in just a few hundred feet. Head south here along the Kettle River and beside the thick sugar maple and basswood trees that line its bank.

A **trail intersection** meets you at 1.3 miles. Across the river is the **River's End canoe camp.** Stay to your right closer to the river at the intersection and continue for another 0.8 mile to the confluence point. The **Two Rivers canoe campsite** marks the spot of the confluence. The upper arm of the St. Croix is dotted with

A stand of birch trees grows tall and narrow.

small islands and sandbars as the Kettle River joins in from the north. Cross the campsite and follow the trail northeast as it now borders the St. Croix River; 1 mile from the campsite, the trail passes an **intersection.** Stay to your right closer to the water and continue heading north. The next 1.1 miles is through the thick of the forest and moves away from the river.

The trail emerges along the park's **gravel road** and crosses over to part of the **Bear Creek Trail.** A mile later, at the 5.2-mile mark, Bear Creek Trail breaks to the right. Take a left at this intersection along **Kennedy Brook.** A mile later, you will cross the gravel road back to the parking lot and trailhead.

Extend the Hike

To walk 2 more miles along the peaceful Kettle River, take a right along the dirt road before crossing over to the parking lot. Cross the park road in 0.3 mile and follow the hiking trail east toward the Kettle River to another overlook point called Kettle River Highbanks. Turn around and return to the parking lot and trailhead to finish the hike.

Directions

From St. Paul, head north on I-35 East for 75.5 miles. Exit right onto MN 48 toward Hinckley for 9.5 miles. Turn right at County Road 21 into the park entrance and follow signs to the Kettle River Overlook for approximately 10 miles. Take a right into the Kettle River Overlook parking lot.

7 DEER CREEK LOOP AND RIVER TRAIL

Wild River State Park, North Branch

Distance: 7.3 miles round-trip

Duration: 4 hours

Elevation Change: 120 feet

Effort: Moderate

Trail: Packed turf, mowed grass, paved, gravel

Users: Hikers, leashed dogs

Season: Year-round

Passes/Fees: $5 daily vehicle permit fee

Maps: Maps available at the park headquarters and on the park website

Contact: Wild River State Park, 39797 Park Trail, Center City, 651/583-2925, www.dnr.state.mn.us, 8am-10pm daily

---

Follow the banks of the St. Croix River.

Wild River State Park has miles of undeveloped shoreline on the St. Croix River.

Start the Hike

From the visitors center parking lot, walk left to the paved **Old Logging Trail** and then take a right onto the packed-dirt footpath that loops around the visitors center building. Take a right at the information and map kiosk to join the **Old Military Road trail.** This wide dirt and gravel path is part of the **Deer Creek Loop;** 0.4 mile from the map kiosk, you will cross an old bridge above Deer Creek where it joins the St. Croix River. Just beyond the bridge is the **Deer Creek canoe campsite.** Continue walking south past the **wooden shelter** for 1 mile along the gravel trail to a trail intersection. Take a right as the trail climbs slightly uphill and begins to head northward through the thick and shady woodland that surrounds Deer Creek. At the top of the loop, take a left back to the **map kiosk.**

Take a right at the next intersection, 0.1 mile away. This trail cuts east toward the river and breaks into an open meadow. Stay to the right at the next trail intersection and follow the river north to the **boat access site.** Cross the gravel road at the boat access and continue north. In a few hundred feet, you will **cross a small creek** and reenter thick forest cover.

You will pass the **Spring Creek canoe campsite** 0.2 mile from the road. In another 0.7 mile, you will reach the **Old Nevers Dam site** and trail intersection.

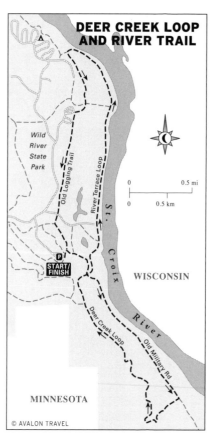

An informational kiosk and history display marks the spot of the old dam.

Continue north from the dam site along the **River Terrace Loop.** Winding wooden steps climb straight up the 60-foot bluff side here. Stay to the left on the trail that leads away from the steps. The stairs are 5.8 miles into the hike. As the trail leads south, it slowly climbs up from the floodplain for 0.5 mile. Go straight at the intersection at the top of the incline on the dirt trail. In 0.2 mile, the dirt path intersects the paved **Old Logging Trail.** This is a straight shot south through the woods and across the boat access park road for 0.7 mile. At the three-way paved intersection, take a left to end up at the visitors center and trailhead just 0.3 mile away.

Hike Nearby

To fit more of a climb into this hike, take a right at the trail intersection at the northern tip of the River Terrace Loop. This trail climbs 164 meandering steps straight up more than 50 feet to the top of the ridge. Turn left at the camper cabins and follow the paved Old Logging Trail back to the visitors center parking lot.

Directions

From St. Paul, head north on I-35 East for 40 miles. Exit right onto MN 96 for 11 miles. Turn left at Maple Lane for 0.2 mile. Turn left onto County Road 12/ Park Trail for 2 miles past the park entrance. Follow signs to the visitors center parking lot.

8 RIVER TRAIL TO SANDSTONE BLUFFS OVERLOOK

Interstate State Park, Taylors Falls

Distance: 3.75 miles round-trip

Duration: 2.5-3 hours

Elevation Change: 250 feet

Effort: Moderate/strenuous

Trail: Packed turf, gravel, rocks

Users: Hikers, leashed dogs

Season: April-November; Sandstone Bluff portion of trail closed in winter

Passes/Fees: $5 daily vehicle permit fee

Maps: Maps available at the park headquarters and on the park website

Contact: Interstate State Park, 307 Milltown Rd., Taylors Fall, 651/465-5711, www.dnr.state.mn.us, 8am-10pm daily

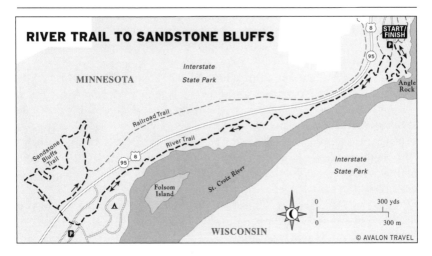

Pick your way through a field of ancient geologic potholes and climb the steep sandstone bluffs that overlook Folsom Island.

Popular for its awesome geologic features, Interstate State Park is also a great hiking destination full of spring ephemeral wildflowers.

© JAKE KULJU

A butterfly plumbs the depths of a Butterfly Weed flower in Interstate State Park.

Start the Hike

Facing the visitors center, take a right toward the pothole field. This 0.25 mile is packed with things to see, including dozens of massive **geologic potholes** and an outlook over the St. Croix River. You won't gain your stride until starting on the River Trail, so take your time around the potholes. Many of them you can climb in and around.

Veer left toward the **Baby Potholes** and take another left toward the **Lily Pond.** Straight south from there, a spur trail leads to an overlook at **Angle Rock.** Return from the overlook and take a left toward the **Bottomless Pit** and **Bake Oven potholes.** More than 60 feet deep, Bottomless Pit is the world's largest explored glacial pothole. At the next trail intersection, keep to the right toward **The Squeeze,** then take another left to the **Caldron.** Return to the main trail and take a right on the trail that runs adjacent to the paved path. Take a left at the interpretive kiosk near the parking lot to join the **River Trail.**

The River Trail meanders 50 feet above the St. Croix and treats you to **two stunning overlooks with views of** the river and Folsom Island.

Just over 1 mile into the hike, the trail descends closer to the water to an **overlook site.** The river bulges around Folsom Island here and provides a beautiful panoramic view of the floodplain forest and wide river. Shortly after the overlook, stay to the right at the trail intersection for another 0.2 mile to a **park road** and parking lot. Turn right here and follow the road past the **park information office** and through a tunnel that runs underneath U.S. Highway 8. On the other side of the highway, the path meets the **Sandstone Bluffs Trail loop.** Walk straight ahead to begin the 200-foot climb to the top up a long and winding set of wooden stairs.

A stunning **overlook** hundreds of feet above the river gives you a commanding view of the surrounding area. The overlook is halfway through the loop, 0.5 mile from the base of the bluff and 3.2 miles into the hike. Continue west before beginning the steep descent to the bottom of a seasonal creek bed. Cross under the highway again toward the park office and follow the **River Trail** back to the parking lot.

Hike Nearby
If you are camping at the park and want to walk into Taylors Falls (the nearby town), take a left up another set of wooden stairs at the bottom of the Sandstone Bluffs Trail loop. This path follows the old railroad tracks for 1.5 miles into town and is just across U.S. Highway 8 from the visitors center parking lot.

Directions
From St. Paul, head north on I-35 East for 25 miles. Exit onto U.S. Highway 8 East for 22 miles. Turn right at MN 95 into the park entrance for 0.2 mile. Follow signs to the visitors center parking lot.

9 PRAIRIE OVERLOOK AND WOODLAND EDGE LOOP

William O'Brien State Park, Marine on St. Croix

Distance: 5.7 miles round-trip

Duration: 2.5-3 hours

Elevation Change: 160 feet

Effort: Moderate

Trail: Mowed grass, packed turf

Users: Hikers, leashed dogs

Season: Year-round; cross-country skiing in winter

Passes/Fees: $5 daily vehicle permit fee

Maps: Maps available at the park headquarters and on the park website

Contact: William O'Brien State Park, 16821 O'Brien Trail North, 651/433-0500, www.dnr.state.mn.us, 8am-10pm daily

---

This hike winds through the ponds and rolling prairie hills of William O'Brien State Park.

The forests, lakes, and grasslands in William O'Brien State Park make for great hiking.

Start the Hike

From the parking lot, walk toward the visitors center and take a left onto the **mowed grass trail** that enters the open, rolling grassland. You will enjoy the vastness of this prairie and wetland

landscape for the next mile before climbing to the **Prairie Overlook Trail.** At 0.2 mile, the trail swings west toward the **Wetland Trail.** Take a left at the next two intersections, 0.1 mile apart, and then a right to stay north of the **Beaver Lodge Trail loop.** The trail hugs the southern edge of a large wetland area in the middle of the park

© JAKE KULJU

The St. Croix River winds through bottomland forest between the hills of William O'Brien State Park.

Take another right 0.2 mile later to keep bordering the wetland. Railroad tracks lie 0.3 mile ahead. Keep going straight to cross the tracks at the next trail intersection and then make a left onto the **Prairie Overlook Trail.** As you begin to climb the 40-foot incline, you will notice how a little elevation makes a big difference in your view. The top of the overlook is 1.8 miles into the hike, marked by a **bench** and lined with coneflowers, Indian paintbrush, and wild daisies.

From the bench, walk northwest for 0.7 mile to the **Woodland Edge Trail** intersection. Take a left onto the forest turf trail, which enters a more heavily wooded area of primarily oak and maple trees. One-third mile after passing a wooden shelter on the Woodland Edge Trail, take a left onto the **Hardwood Hills Trail,** which arcs through a thickly wooded, rolling landscape for 0.8 mile, climbing 40 feet back to the Woodland Edge Trail. Taking a left at the next two trail intersections brings you to a **tunnel** that passes underneath the train tracks. From here the forest path descends back into the large wetland area and **Savanna Campground.** Dotted with small ponds, the 0.9 mile from the tunnel leads to the **Wetland Trail.** Take a left at this intersection back to the visitors center and parking lot.

Extend the Hike

Head east from the visitors center along the trail that follows the park road down to the river. A trail makes a loop past Lake Alice and Greenberg Island in the St. Croix. This will add 4.2 miles and 100 feet to your hike, making it a challenging all-day outing.

Directions

From St. Paul, head north on I-35 East for 16 miles. Turn right onto County Road 14 for 0.6 mile. Continue on Frenchman Road North for 1.4 miles. Turn left at Forest Boulevard North for 2.8 miles. Turn right at 170th Street North for 8.2 miles. Continue on Ostrium Trail North for 2.8 miles. Turn left at Broadway Street for 0.4 mile. Turn left at Maple Street and make a quick left onto St. Croix Trail North for 2 miles. Turn left at O'Brien Trail North and follow signs to the visitors center.

10 EAGLE POINT LAKE TRAIL

Lake Elmo Park Reserve, Lake Elmo

Distance: 4.5 miles round-trip

Duration: 2.5-3 hours

Elevation Change: Negligible

Effort: Easy/moderate

Trail: Dirt, mowed grass

Users: Hikers

Season: Year-round; cross-country and skate skiing in winter

Passes/Fees: $5 daily vehicle permit fee

Maps: Maps available on the park website

Contact: Lake Elmo Park Reserve, 1515 Keats Avenue, 651/430-8370, www. co.washington.mn.us, 6am-10pm daily

Circumnavigate Eagle Point Lake and its extensive grasslands.

Wide-open expanses surround Eagle Point Lake and make for excellent prairie hiking in spring and summer.

Start the Hike

Facing Eagle Point Lake from the large paved parking lot, take a right onto the **dirt trail** heading north. The trail cuts west on one of the lake's large peninsulas and then breaks into open grassland when it makes a sharp turn to the right. The trail crosses a **land bridge** between the lake and a smaller pond. At the **intersection** on the other side, take a left along the tree line that hugs the lake. A narrow swath of mostly maple trees borders the water for 0.5 mile up along the northernmost arm of the lake. As the trail arcs around the northern tip of the water, it enters the expansive grasslands that dominate the landscape. Turning to the south, the trail briefly enters another stand of trees.

© JAKE KULJU

an open meadow and a big sky near Eagle Point Lake

At the upcoming **trail intersection,** make a sharp right that leads north out of the stand of trees and into the rolling prairie hills. At **marker 26,** keep left as the trail arcs south through the prairie for 0.4 mile. Almost 2 miles from the trailhead, you reach **marker 27.** Choose the middle path here and continue walking south. The grassy trail eventually veers east and rejoins **Eagle Point Lake** at its wooded southern shore.

The tree cover soon becomes scarce in 0.2 mile and clears to prairie again. Take a left at the next trail intersection and follow the eastern shore of the lake to **marker 19.** Take the second right at this junction in just a few hundred feet, along the grassy trail that arcs back up to the parking lot. Note that lights are turned on for night hiking, as well.

Shorten the Hike

For a shorter hike that stays closer to the lake, turn left and continue going south at marker 28. Keep closer to the water by taking a left at marker 29, as well. This will shave 0.75 mile off your hike.

Directions

From St. Paul, take I-94 East for 8.8 miles. Exit left onto Keats Avenue for 1.7 miles. Keats Avenue leads right to the park entrance. Follow signs to the Eagle Point Lake parking lot 0.2 mile ahead on your left.

11 ST. CROIX RIVER TRAIL
Afton State Park, Hastings

Distance: 4 miles round-trip

Duration: 2-2.5 hours

Elevation Change: 180 feet

Effort: Moderate

Trail: Paved, packed turf, mowed grass, gravel

Users: Hikers, cyclists, horse riders, leashed dogs

Season: Year-round

Passes/Fees: $5 daily vehicle permit fee

Maps: Maps available at the visitors center and on the park website

Contact: Afton State Park, 6959 Peller Avenue South, Hastings, 651/436-5391, www.dnr.state.mn.us, 8am-10pm daily

---

Shoreline views and bluff-top vistas await along the St. Croix River Trail in Afton State Park.

Just a half hour drive from St. Paul, Afton occupies a choice piece of land in the St. Croix River Valley full of bluff-top views and rocky shoreline.

Start the Hike
The trailhead begins at the **visitors center** and heads south. Take a right onto the paved **hiker/cyclist trail** that runs between the center and the parking lot. Stay right at the first intersection behind the visitors center to join the **Hiking Club trail.** In a few hundred feet, an **interpretive trail** makes a 0.5-mile loop through one of Afton's prairie restoration areas.

After passing the Richard Naegeli memorial bench and completing the prairie loop, cross the paved path and take a right onto the mowed-grass **horse/hiking trail.** Follow this wide trail through the grasslands on top of the bluff for 0.3 mile to the 1-mile **overlook hiking trail** that heads east. Take a left onto the narrower path as it gently descends 60 feet to an overlook on the edge of the bluff.

From the **overlook,** the path meanders south for 0.8 mile past a **group campsite** and across two park roads. This trail leads past a **wooden shelter** 0.2 mile from the next intersection. Take a left when you reach it, heading into the thick oak, maple, and basswood forest that hugs the bluff side near the river.

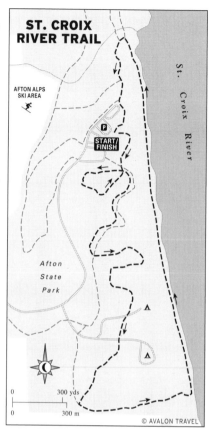

The **gravel hiking path** becomes quite steep near the river, dropping 120 feet in 0.1 mile. Use extra caution on wet days or after rainfall, as the path can be slippery. At the bottom of the bluff, the trail swings north on a wide, straight gravel path along the riverbank for 1.7 miles. You will have several opportunities to approach the water from the gravel. The trail is approximately 20 feet above the river, but several sets of overgrown **wooden and stone stairways** lead through the brush down to the water.

At the end of the 1.7-mile stretch, the paved **hiker/cyclist path** cuts sharply to your left. Start taking this up the hill and then veer to the left onto the narrower gravel **Hiking Club trail.** This climb through the forest gives you another overlook and ends in 0.2 mile when it rejoins the paved path. Follow the paved trail for 0.2 mile back to the visitors center.

Options

To make the steep climb at the southern end of this trail early in your hike, simply reverse your route, but be prepared for an intense uphill climb. Use caution, especially on wet days.

Directions

From St. Paul, take I-94 East for 11 miles. Exit right onto County Road 95 South for 7 miles. Turn left at 70th Street South for 3.5 miles to the park entrance. Follow signs to the visitors center another 1.8 miles ahead.

12 KINNI CANYON TRAIL

Glen Park, River Falls, Wisconsin

Best: River Hikes

Distance: 3.7 miles round-trip

Duration: 2.5-3 hours

Elevation Change: 60 feet

Effort: Moderate

Trail: Gravel, packed turf, dirt

Users: Hikers, leashed dogs

Season: Year-round

Passes/Fees: None

Maps: Maps available on the land trust website

Contact: Kinnickinnic River Land Trust, 421 North Main Street, 715/425-5738, www.kinniriver.org, dawn-dusk daily

---

Explore the banks of the Kinnickinnic River in western Wisconsin.

The trail along this lovely, meandering river starts at Glen Park in River Falls, Wisconsin. Known to locals as Kinni Creek, this river is also a fly-fishing hot spot.

Start the Hike

From the parking lot, walk around the tennis courts to the wide tree-lined path that leads to the **dam.** Take a left and follow the **gravel trail** along the bank of the river.

From **Glen Park,** the path makes a 0.4-mile arc to the south. The gravel path here, lined with benches and mowed grass, is easy walking from the dam. Another wide **gravel walking path** joins the riverbank trail 0.4 mile in, and then quickly narrows into a packed **dirt pathway.** From here, the narrow path turns into a kind of delta of walkways. Small forest paths and packed dirt trails all head in the same general direction but crisscross each other and branch around different obstacles as they follow the river. Choose whichever path you'd like. It is almost impossible

© JAKE KULJU

Trees and heavy brush overhang the quick-moving waters of the Kinnickinnic River.

to get lost, as no path leads far from the water, and the trees aren't thick enough to block your sight of it.

After 0.3 mile of flowing south, the river makes a sharp turn to the north, and the trail follows it. The water splits around several shallow islands and sandbars here for 0.1 mile; then makes another run to the south at the **0.5-mile mark.** Just before the top of this northern arc, the path narrows to a small **dirt footpath** that climbs the side of a steep bank. This only lasts a few hundred feet before the trail drops back to the water's edge. The river makes a quick southern turn 0.2 mile from the steep bank, creating a deep pool at the point of a horn-shaped piece of land.

The trail becomes narrower over the next 0.25 mile. Before the next river bend, the brush becomes too thick for recreational hiking. You can walk in the water to go farther, or turn back to the trailhead.

Extend the Hike
A trail runs along the other side of the creek as well. At Glen Park, you can choose one path or return and take them both to lengthen your hike.

Directions
From St. Paul, take I-94 East for 19 miles into Wisconsin. Exit onto WI 35 South toward River Falls for 7.2 miles. Take the River Falls ramp onto North Main Street for 2.2 miles. Turn right at West Park Street and right again onto Glen Park Road and the Glen Park parking lot.

13 COTTAGE GROVE RAVINE TRAILS

Cottage Grove Ravine Regional Park, Cottage Grove

Distance: 2.8 miles round-trip

Duration: 2.5 hours

Elevation Change: 150 feet

Effort: Moderate

Trail: Packed turf, mowed grass, paved

Users: Hikers, cyclists, leashed dogs

Season: Year-round; cross-country skiing in winter

Passes/Fees: $5 daily vehicle permit fee

Maps: Maps available at the trailhead and on the park website

Contact: Cottage Grove Ravine Regional Park, 9940 Point Douglas Road, 763/694-7650, www.co.washington.mn.us, 7am-9pm daily

---

Walk through the Cottage Grove Ravine.

Follow a thickly forested path through a deep glacial ravine.

Start the Hike

Walk toward the kiosk to the right of the picnic pavilion and follow the **forest turf trail** that leads right. This wide, oak-lined path gently climbs through the forest along the eastern edge of the park. Each intersection is marked with a numbered wooden post. You will come to **marker 2** at 0.4 mile from the trailhead. Take a right and walk down a small hill to a **service road.** Power lines run through the park here, and the trail briefly follows the area where trees have been cleared. The road is quite overgrown and is more of a wide trail than a gravel road. Take another right at **marker 5.** The trail continues a gradual climb here through oak and maple trees for 0.1 mile and then abruptly enters an open field. The trail bends to the west on its way to **marker 8.**

Take a right here and follow the **grassy hilltop trail** to a denser pine forest. In a few hundred feet, you will come to **marker 9.** Veer to the right once again onto a narrow forest turf path.

Marker 12 is the halfway point, 1.4 miles from the trailhead. Take a sharp left onto the **paved hiker/cyclist** trail and follow it as it meanders south through the bottom of the ravine.

At **marker 16,** the trail bends south toward Cottage Grove Ravine Pond and follows its eastern shore. **Marker 17** is at the fishing pier that overlooks the pond and the rising hill on the other side of the park. Continue on the paved path to the picnic pavilion and parking loop.

Extend the Hike

To explore more of the ravine, take a left at trail marker 2 to marker 4; then take a right and walk north, taking a left at trail marker 7. When you get to trail marker 8, you'll be at the 0.75-mile point in the trail description with 0.25-mile more under your belt.

Directions

From St. Paul, take Shepard Road East to Warner Road for 2.5 miles. Merge right onto U.S. Highway 10 East/U.S. Highway 61 South for 13 miles. Exit left onto Innovation Road and take a right onto East Point Douglas Road South for 0.5 mile. Turn left into the park entrance. Stay to your right after the fee station and park in the picnic shelter parking loop.

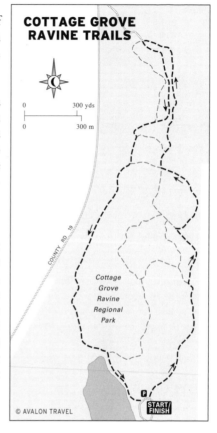

COTTAGE GROVE RAVINE TRAILS

0   300 yds

0   300 m

COUNTY RD 19

Cottage Grove Ravine Regional Park

START/FINISH

© AVALON TRAVEL

14 VERMILLION FALLS TRAIL

Vermillion Falls Park, Hastings

Distance: 4.6 miles round-trip

Duration: 2.5 hours

Elevation Change: Negligible

Effort: Easy/moderate

Trail: Paved, packed turf

Users: Hikers, wheelchair users, leashed dogs

Season: Year-round

Passes/Fees: None

Maps: Maps available on the park website

Contact: Vermillion Falls Park, 215 21st Street East, 651/480-6175, www.hastingsmn.gov, sunrise-sunset daily

Walk from Vermillion Falls, near the Old Mill Ruins, to Bull Frog Pond.

Vermillion Falls Park in Hastings wraps along the eastern edge of the city near the confluence of the Mississippi, St. Croix, and Vermillion Rivers. This paved trail is a great place to take children for a weekend outing.

Start the Hike

This hike starts with a spectacular view of **Vermillion Falls.** From the parking lot, walk straight ahead toward the river. A small **pavilion** is behind the trees that line the Vermillion River at the foot of the falls. Follow the river downstream to your right on the **paved path.** The trail heads east and follows the upper bank of the **Vermillion River** as it heads towards its confluence with the St. Croix and Mississippi Rivers; 0.4 mile from the falls, the paved trail turns left and crosses high above the river. High stone cliffs make a small gorge here that is full of the sounds of splashing water and chirping birds.

At the **bridge**, the trail leads north along a tree-lined path. A half mile after the bridge, the trail juts left and then runs parallel to **Tyler Street.** At the **8th Street** intersection, cross the road to the right and follow the paved path toward **Bull Frog Pond.** The path crosses over the Vermillion River again and leads to **C. P. Adams Park,** about 1 mile ahead on the southern shore of the pond. Follow the looped path around the perimeter of the clearing and head back to the trailhead the way you came. When crossing over the high bridge back to **Vermillion Falls Park,** you will see the other side of the ravine and the small cascades that fall through the rocks. When you reach **Vermillion Falls,** take a left after the pavilion to return to the parking lot.

The Vermillion River gorge in Hastings is rife with rock outcroppings and red pine trees.

Extend the Hike

You can continue on the southern shore of the Vermillion River past the high bridge on a packed dirt trail to add 0.5 mile to this hike and view the Old Mill Ruins. The trail follows the top of the ravine and leaves the park. An old mill building with an informational kiosk stands 0.25 mile from the bridge. Turn around and take a right over the high bridge to continue the hike.

Directions

From St. Paul, take Shepard Road East to Warner Road for 2.5 miles. Merge right onto U.S. Highway 10 East/U.S. Highway 61 South for 18 miles. Continue on Vermillion Street for 1.3 miles after entering Hastings. Turn left at 21st Street East for 0.2 mile into the Vermillion Falls parking lot on your left.

15 LAKE PEPIN OVERLOOK HIKING CLUB TRAIL

Frontenac State Park, Frontenac

Best: Views

Distance: 3.3 miles round-trip

Duration: 2 hours

Elevation Change: 220 feet

Effort: Moderate

Trail: Packed turf

Users: Hikers, leashed dogs

Season: Year-round

Passes/Fees: $5 daily vehicle permit fee

Maps: Maps available at the park office and on the park website

Contact: Frontenac State Park, 29223 County 28 Boulevard, 651/345-3401, www.dnr.state.mn.us, 8am-10pm daily

---

Views of the Mississippi River's most popular lake and surrounding bluffs are impressive along this clifftop trail.

Hiking above Lake Pepin, you'll be able to take in the beauty of the lake and the surrounding high bluffs.

Start the Hike

From the parking loop adjacent to the park office, head east into the rolling prairie. The grassy path joins the **Hiking Club trail** 0.3 mile from the trailhead. Take the left branch as it begins to climb uphill into the oak and maple forest. One mile into the trail, take a right and follow the **Hiking Club** signs for another 0.5 mile to the top of the bluff. The trail crosses the paved park road and veers to the right toward a mowed **picnic area** that overlooks the small town of Frontenac and shimmering **Lake Pepin.**

The **Hiking Club trail** skirts the parking lot near the picnic area and then makes a slight dip down to the edge of the bluff. Follow the trail as it hugs the cliffside and gives you two stunning **overlook points.** A half mile from the picnic area, the trail heads west and zigzags to the south out of the trees and back into the rolling prairie grasses. At the intersection, stay left to return to the trailhead and parking lot near the park office.

Extend the Hike

If you've got strong legs, you might want to add 1.3 miles and 250 feet to this hike. After crossing the park road, take a left and head west toward In Yan Teopa Rock. This trail slides down the bluff and cuts back east nearer the lake, and then climbs a brutal 250 feet in 0.1 mile up to the Hiking Club trail.

Directions

From St. Paul, take Shepard Road East to Warner Road for 2.5 miles. Merge right onto U.S. Highway 10 East/U.S. Highway 61 South for 16 miles. Follow U.S. Highway 10 left into Wisconsin for 3.2 miles. Turn right at Broad Street North in Prescott and continue on WI 35 for 19 miles. Turn right onto U.S. Highway 63 into Minnesota for 3 miles. Turn right at Potter Street in Red Wing and turn right onto U.S. Highway 61 for 10 miles. Turn left at County 2 Boulevard for 1 mile. Turn left at County 28 Boulevard for 1 mile to the park entrance. Park at the park office parking lot.

16 RIVERBEND TRAIL

Carley State Park, Altura

Best: Viewing Wildlife

Distance: 3.1 miles round-trip

Duration: 2 hours

Elevation Change: 350 feet

Effort: Moderate/strenuous

Trail: Packed turf, stone, concrete blocks

Users: Hikers, leashed dogs

Season: Year-round

Passes/Fees: $5 daily vehicle permit fee

Maps: Maps available at the park office and on the park website

Contact: Carley State Park, c/o Whitewater State Park, 19041 Hwy 74, Altura, 507/932-3007, www.dnr.state.mn.us, 8am-10pm daily

---

This pine forest trail climbs up and down a curving river gorge.

Tucked into a quiet river bend of the Whitewater River, this little-used trail will give you 350 feet of river gorge climbing.

Start the Hike

As you head north from the parking lot into the woods, you will notice tall, thick stands of red and white pine. Take a left at the **first trail intersection** just 75 feet ahead and another left in 0.1 mile; 300 feet ahead, take a right at the trail intersection onto a **forest turf path** that leads to a long set of moss-covered stone steps. They descend 80 feet and can be slippery. After taking the steps, you will be in the bottom of the ravine. Follow the trail as it winds north, and take a right at the trail crossing that leads to the river. A series of **concrete blocks** spans the water. You have to jump from block to block to make it across. During high water this can be nearly impossible, and you may want to use a walking stick for balance even when the water is low.

Take a left after crossing the concrete blocks and walk back up the other side of the ravine to the top of the eastern ridge. Take a left at the trail crossing 0.4 mile from the bridge. The trail deposits you at a **river crossing** with more concrete blocks. On the other side, take a left at the trail crossing and another left in 0.1 mile.

A right would lead you to the **camp-ground area.** The next stretch of trail leads 0.4 mile along the riverbank in the bottom of the gorge. The temperature can often be 5-10 degrees cooler in the ravine than in surrounding areas.

When you reach the **first river crossing point,** go south on the trail you took to get there. After you climb the stone steps, take a left at the next **two trail crossings.** You will be back in the thick pine forest again. Take another left to visit an **outlook** point 600 feet from the last intersection. Return to the main trail from the overlook and take a left to return to the trailhead and parking lot just over 500 feet ahead.

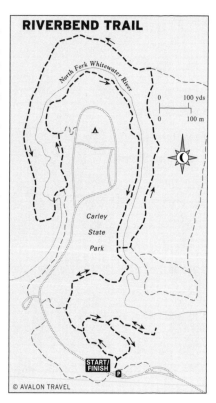

Extend the Hike

To delve deeper into the woods on the east side of the river and add 0.4 mile to your hike, take a right after the river's first crossing point and follow a trail that arcs east up and over the ridge, then north, then west back to the main trail.

Directions

From St. Paul, take U.S. Highway 52 South for 6.2 miles. Exit to continue on U.S. Highway 52 South for another 56 miles. Turn left onto County Road 12 and continue on MN 247 for 19.5 miles. Turn right at MN 42 for 0.5 mile. Turn left onto County Road 4 for 3.2 miles. Take a right into the park entrance and drive 0.1 mile to the trailhead parking lot just past the park office.

17 DAKOTA AND TROUT RUN CREEK TRAILS

Whitewater State Park, Altura

Best: Views

Distance: 6.7 miles round-trip

Duration: 4.5 hours

Elevation Change: 400 feet

Effort: Strenuous

Trail: Dirt, packed turf, wooden steps, rocks, gravel road

Users: Hikers, leashed dogs

Season: Year-round; stairs to Inspiration Point closed in winter

Passes/Fees: $5 daily vehicle permit fee

Maps: Maps available at the park office and on the park website

Contact: Whitewater State Park, 19041 Hwy 74, Altura, 507/932-3007, www.dnr.state.mn.us, 8am-10pm daily

This hike traverses a steep river bluff trail.

From the climb to Inspiration Point to the descent to the bottomlands along Trout Run Creek, this is one of the most challenging and entertaining hikes in the state.

Start the Hike

Begin by walking around the **Nature Store** and following the **dirt trail** that leads uphill straight away from the parking lot. This is the beginning of the **Dakota Trail,** which loops around the Whitewater River to the west.

The trail quickly climbs up to the top of the ridge. Take a right at the next two trail intersections to stay on the Dakota Trail. Oak and maple trees dominate this forested area, providing shade in the summer and blazing colors in autumn. The trail ascends and descends along the ridge over the next 0.9 miles. Take two right-hand turns to cross the river, followed shortly by a left, all in the next 0.2-mile stretch. The Dakota Trail makes one sharp switchback turn on the western bluff and then heads south toward **Signal Point.** This spur trail is barely 0.1 mile long and gives a beautiful view of the river as it flows east.

Return to the main trail and take a left. The trail climbs another 100 feet in 0.5 mile to **Eagle Point overlook.** Take a right at Eagle Point and follow the Dakota Trail southeast as it gently descends to MN 74. Cross the road and continue east up another bluff and down a switchback back to the river. Take a right before the bridge onto **Trout Run Creek Trail.**

Rocky Inspiration Point juts out from the trees high above Trout Run Creek.

Deep in the valley and sandwiched between two 200-foot bluffs, this trail feels like walking in the bottom of a lush and narrow canyon. At 0.4 mile from the bridge, take a left onto the **Inspiration Point spur trail.** This path begins climbing the bluff and then leads to several sets of steep **wooden staircases** with hundreds of steps leading straight up the bluff. At the top, turn to your left on the narrow **rock path.** Cedar trees cling to the rocks and sprout from the boulders. The trail leads to a narrow outcropping of rock that juts into the air. The entire park and its lush forests, rolling bluff tops, and winding river lie more than 200 feet straight below. Note that if you're afraid of heights, you may not be able to stomach the view.

Make your way back to **Trout Run Creek Trail** and take a left for 0.6 mile to the turnaround loop at the trail's end. This creek trail gets wild in some places, as it isn't often traveled. Several **wooden bridges** cross different branches of the creek. The narrow dirt path can be lost sometimes in the overhanging brush, so keep your eyes open. After returning to the bridge at the head of Trout Run Creek Trail, take a right and cross the river on the trail that follows the gravel road back to the parking lot at the Nature Store.

Shorten the Hike

After returning down the rock path on spur trail, simply take a right (skipping Trout Creek) to finish the hike and shave off a mile.

Directions

From St. Paul, take U.S. Highway 52 South for 6.2 miles. Exit to continue on U.S. Highway 52 South for another 56 miles. Turn left onto County Road 12 and continue on MN 247 for 19.5 miles. Turn right at MN 42 for 0.5 mile. Turn left onto County Road 4 for 3.5 miles. Continue on County Road 10 for another 3.5 miles. Turn left at County Road 2 for 3 miles. Continue on County Road 39 for 2.5 miles. Turn right at MN 74 for 0.3 mile to the Nature Store parking lot.

18 RIVERVIEW TRAIL TO BLUFFTOP TRAIL

Perrot State Park, Trempealeau, Wisconsin

Best: Views

Distance: 4.5 miles round-trip

Duration: 3 hours

Elevation Change: 420 feet

Effort: Strenuous

Trail: Dirt, packed turf

Users: Hikers, leashed dogs

Season: Year-round; partial cross-country ski route in winter

Passes/Fees: $5 resident vehicle permit fee ($10 nonresident fee)

Maps: Maps available at the park office and nature center

Contact: Perrot State Park, 26247 Sullivan Rd., Trempealeau, 608/534-6409, www.dnr.state.wi.us, 6am-11pm daily

---

Stunning vistas of the towering bluffs along this portion of the Mississippi are plentiful in Perrot State Park.

The trails in Perrot State Park from the riverbank to the rising bluffs give hikers views of the rolling bluff landscape in Minnesota and the wild Wisconsin forests that dominate the park.

Start the Hike

Begin hiking south from the nature center parking lot by walking behind the building and taking a left near the water. The **dirt path** follows the eastern edge of Trempealeau Bay, where the Trempealeau River forms a confluence with the Mississippi River. The trail passes directly by an ancient **Indian burial mound.** Signs give some history of the site. Keep walking south to the picnic area and bay **overlook point.** Looking west, you will see Trempealeau Mountain rising like a volcanic island at the confluence point of the two rivers.

A dragonfly basks in the sun.

The trail crosses the **boat landing road** and parking lot 0.3 mile from the lookout point. Cross the road and follow the trail south toward the Mississippi River. The **Riverview Trail** runs between the park road and the railroad tracks that skirt the riverbank. At 1.5 miles from the trailhead, choose the **middle trail option,** which crosses the parking loop and park road, heading northeast. This begins the **blufftop trail** that leads farther into the forest away from the water and climbs the park's highest bluffs. The trail starts climbing to **Reed's Peak** about 0.6 mile from the park road crossing. At the top of the bluff, the trail arcs west to the **Perrot Ridge overlook** point. This high point looks over the river and gives views of Brady's Bluff and the Minnesota bluff line.

The trail quickly descends a steep slope to the base of the bluff and crosses a **ski trail.** Keep going south for 0.4 mile toward the park road and stay to the right at the trail intersection near the road. The **forest turf trail** winds through the oak woods for 0.6 mile before climbing **Brady's Bluff.** At the top of Brady's Bluff, a **ski shelter** is near the overlook point. Take a left back down the bluff toward the boat landing. Cross the road and walk through the parking lot toward the water and picnic area. Here you rejoin the Riverview Trail. Take a right to head back to the nature center parking lot.

Shorten the Hike

You can take in the grandeur of the bluffs without climbing all of them. The Riverview Trail provides sweeping views of the river valley and the bluffs on both sides of the river and will turn this into a 2.7-mile hike. Just turn around at the parking loop and follow the trail along the river back to the nature center.

Directions

From St. Paul, take U.S. Highway 52 South for 6.2 miles. Exit to continue on U.S. Highway 52 South for another 76.5 miles. Turn left to merge onto I-90 East toward Lacrosse for 34 miles. Exit left onto MN 43 toward Winona for 7 miles. Follow MN 43 for 2 miles through Winona to the MN 43/WI 54 bridge that crosses the Mississippi into Wisconsin. Turn right onto WI 54 for 6 miles. Turn right at West Prairie Road for 3.8 miles. Turn right at Lehmann Road for 0.5 mile.

19 KING'S AND QUEEN'S BLUFF TRAIL

Great River Bluffs State Park, Winona

Best: Views

Distance: 4.5 miles round-trip

Duration: 2.5-3 hours

Elevation Change: 220 feet

Effort: Moderate

Trail: Mowed grass, packed turf

Users: Hikers, leashed dogs

Season: Year-round

Passes/Fees: $5 daily vehicle permit fee

Maps: Maps available at the park office and on the park website

Contact: Great River Bluffs State Park, 43605 Kipp Drive, 507/643-6849, www.dnr.state.mn.us, 8am-10pm daily

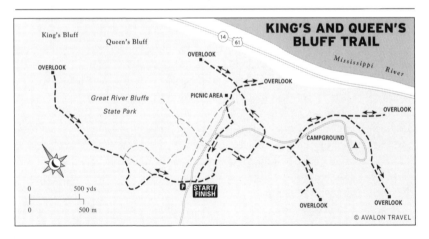

This awe-inspiring hike tours bluffs high above the Mississippi River.

Home of King's and Queen's Bluffs, this park offers views of the river valley and undulating landscape that are fit for royalty.

© JAKE KULJU

The grassy sides of Queen's Bluff rise from the Mississippi River Valley.

Start the Hike

Facing north with the parking lot at your back, take a right, crossing the road and starting east on the **mowed grass trail.** Stay to your right at the **first trail intersection** less than 0.1 mile ahead. This trail section slides along the open bluff side.

Take rights at the next **two trail crossings.** The path continues through the grassy landscape interspersed with prairie shrubs and trees on its way to the group camp parking lot. Follow the trail behind the parking area to the **Pioneer Group Camp site.** Two overlook points branch off from the campsite and give views to the lush valley below. Return to the maintenance building area and take a right on the trail on the other side of the park road. This leads you into the pine forest and farther east toward the campground parking lot. Take a left at the parking lot toward another **overlook point,** and then return the way you came all the way back to the group camp parking area. Stay to your right and take another right at the upcoming **trail crossing.**

You will climb approximately 50 feet to the **picnic area.** Take a left on the trail that leads to an overlook point on the eastern edge of **Queen's Bluff.** No trail leads to Queen's Bluff, but you can see it jutting out over the valley from the overlook point. Return to the picnic area and walk across the parking lot to the trail that follows the road back to the place you parked. Take a right here to join the **interpretive trail.** This is the most scenic part of the hike and will take you to the end of **King's Bluff.** The mowed grass path skirts the northern edge of a grassland and enters a thick stand of pine trees. Follow the packed-dirt and forest turf trail when it enters the trees all the way to the open grassland on the end of King's Bluff. Head back to the parking lot along the interpretive trail.

Shorten the Hike

If you want a great view without stopping at every overlook in the park, take the 1.5-mile interpretive trail out to King's Bluff and back. This is the most popular trail, and it leads to the most sweeping view of both the river valley and of Queen's Bluff.

Directions

From St. Paul, take U.S. Highway 52 South for 6.2 miles. Exit to continue on U.S. Highway 52 South for another 76.5 miles. Turn left to merge onto I-90 East toward Lacrosse for 48 miles. Turn left onto County Road 12 and take a quick right in 0.2 mile onto County Road 3 for 1 mile. Turn right at Lynch Road for 2 miles past the park entrance to the interpretive trail parking lot.

MISSISSIPPI RIVER VALLEY AND SOUTHERN MINNESOTA

© JAKE KULJU

Trails in the valley offer the best of Minnesota's wetlands, Big Woods forests, and wildlife. A few miles from St. Paul, the Minnesota Valley National Wildlife Refuge covers more than 14,000 acres of land. One hundred different species of birds nest here, including great blue herons, bald eagles, and tundra swans. Even the most remote places have some access trails, allowing hikers to observe rare and beautiful wildlife.

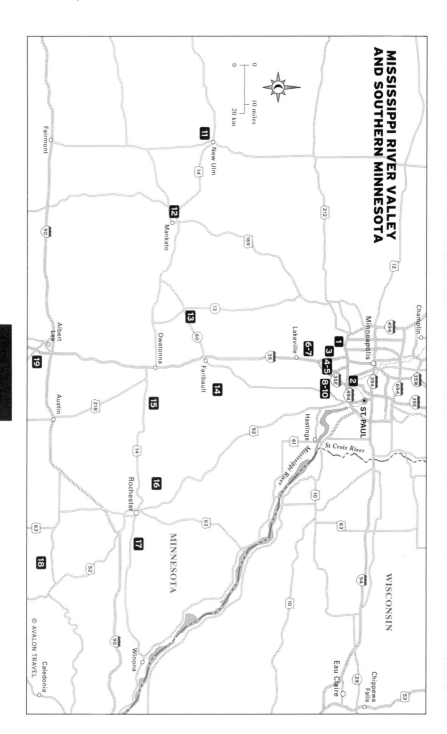

TRAIL NAME	LEVEL	DISTANCE	TIME	ELEVATION	PAGE
1 Hyland and Bush Lakes Loop	Easy/moderate	4.5 mi rt	2.5–3 hr	Negligible	172
2 Pike Island Loop	Easy	3.5 mi rt	1.5–2 hr	Negligible	174
3 Wilkie Rookery Trail	Moderate	6.1 mi rt	3.5 hr	Negligible	176
4 Louisville Swamp Loop	Moderate	5.7 mi rt	3 hr	100 ft	178
5 Black Dog Lake Trail	Easy	4 mi rt	2 hr	Negligible	180
6 Hanrehan Lake Trail	Easy/moderate	5.1 mi rt	2.5 hr	10 ft	182
7 Murphy Lake to Minnregs Lake Trail	Moderate	6.3 mi rt	3–3.5 hr	100 ft	184
8 Western Lebanon Hills Hiking Trail	Easy	2.5 mi rt	1.5 hr	60 ft	186
9 Jensen Lake Trail	Easy	3.3 mi rt	2 hr	60 ft	188
10 Holland and O'Brien Lakes Trail	Moderate	4.6 mi rt	3 hr	70 ft	190
11 Cottonwood River and Hiking Club Trail	Moderate/strenuous	5.6 mi rt	3 hr	210 ft	193
12 Seppman Windmill Trail	Easy	4 mi rt	2 hr	50 ft	196
13 Big Woods Loop to Timber Doodle Trail	Moderate/strenuous	6.1 mi rt	3–3.5 hr	270 ft	198
14 Hidden Falls to Hope Trail Loop	Easy/moderate	4.7 mi rt	2.5 hr	90 ft	201
15 Rice Lake Trail	Easy	3.5 mi rt	1.75 hr	Negligible	204
16 Zumbro River and High Meadow Trail	Moderate	5.1 mi rt	2.75 hr	120 ft	206
17 North Trail, Prairie Ridge Trail, and the Dam Overlook	Moderate	5.6 mi rt	3 hr	100 ft	208
18 Sugar Camp Hollow and Big Spring Trail	Strenuous	11.8 mi rt	7–8 hr	520 ft	210
19 Big Island to Great Marsh Trail	Easy/moderate	6 mi rt	3 hr	Negligible	213

1 HYLAND AND BUSH LAKES LOOP

Hyland Lake Park Reserve, Bloomington

Distance: 4.5 miles round-trip

Duration: 2.5-3 hours

Elevation Change: Negligible

Effort: Easy/moderate

Trail: Packed turf, gravel, paved

Users: Hikers, cyclists, leashed dogs

Season: Year-round

Passes/Fees: None

Maps: Maps available at the park office and on the park website

Contact: Hyland Lake Park Reserve, 10145 Bush Lake Road, 763/694-7687, www.threeriverspark.org, 5am-10pm daily

Enjoy a lakeside hike through mature hardwood forests and an open prairie.

Hyland Lake Park Reserve, in the heart of Bloomington, has some of the most breathtaking prairie trails in the southern half of the state.

Start the Hike

Begin by walking behind the visitors center toward **Hyland Lake.** Take a right as you near the water and head south toward the fishing pier. The **turf trail** follows the oak-lined lakeshore around the western arm of Hyland Lake and then delves into the thicker forest that covers the southern and eastern shores. Take a right at the first trail intersection and cross over the **paved hiker/cyclist path.** A **drinking fountain** marks this intersection, 0.4 mile from the trailhead.

Keep to the right at the next trail intersection and follow the turf trail as it arcs through the park's southern forest and around one of the park's small ponds. One mile from the drinking fountain, take a right at the **turf trail intersection** and head north along Hyland Lake's eastern shore. The trail runs parallel to a set of train tracks and comes quite close to them on the eastern end of the lake. Take another right at the northern end of the lake and you will soon break out of the forest into the broad prairie meadows that Hyland Lake Park Reserve is known for.

After another right-hand turn, you come to a **four-way intersection.** Take the middle path, which leads north and crosses the paved hiker/cyclist path; 0.2 mile from the paved intersection, the trail meets a **gravel road** that leads to the

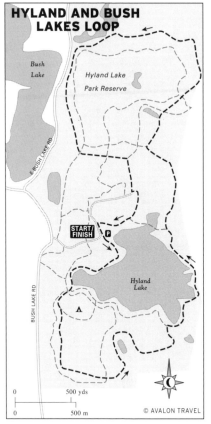

maintenance facility. Turn left and follow the turf trail west here for 0.6 mile to another intersection with the paved hiker/cyclist trail. This 0.6-mile stretch passes through an open prairie corridor between two stands of trees. At the **paved intersection,** take a left on the turf trail into the heart of the prairie.

In 0.6 mile, take a left on the **gravel road** that leads east to a parking lot on your right. At the intersection with the **paved hiker/cyclist path,** take a left and follow the pavement south toward the lake and past the visitors center. Leave the trail at the visitors center and find the parking lot on the other side of the building.

Hike Nearby

Another turf trail near the Bush Lake trail intersection leads north to the Richardson Nature Center trail system. Turn right at Bush Lake to enter the interpretive trails that surround the ponds, forests, and prairie of the park's northern section.

Directions

From Minneapolis, take I-35 West south for 7.2 miles. Merge onto I-494 West for 2.7 miles. Exit left onto East Bush Lake Road for 0.5 mile. Turn right to continue on East Bush Lake Road for another 2.4 miles. Turn left at Highland Lake Park Road for 0.2 mile to the visitors center parking lot.

2 PIKE ISLAND LOOP

Fort Snelling State Park, St. Paul

🦌 🐕 👪 ♿

Best: Historical Hikes, River Hikes

Distance: 3.5 miles round-trip

Duration: 1.5-2 hours

Elevation Change: Negligible

Effort: Easy

Trail: Paved, packed turf

Users: Hikers, wheelchair users, leashed dogs

Season: Year-round

Passes/Fees: $5 daily vehicle permit fee

Maps: Maps available at the park office and on the park website

Contact: Fort Snelling State Park, 101 Snelling Lake Rd., 612/725-2724, www. dnr.state.mn.us, 8am-10pm daily

Make an easy loop around the confluence of the Minnesota and Mississippi Rivers.

Fort Snelling is on the bluff high above the confluence of the Mississippi and Minnesota Rivers. The best trail in the park, however, is down below on the island where the waters meet.

PIKE ISLAND LOOP

Start the Hike

From the parking lot, walk north to the **visitors center** to get some historical background on the area. The visitors center also has detailed maps of the area.

From the visitors center, follow the **paved walking path** east. Signs indicate the direction of Pike Island. Cross the **footbridge** to the island and take a right onto the smooth, packed **dirt and turf trail.**

You will come to two **trail intersections** on the south side of the island. Keep straight ahead at each one to complete a full loop around the island. At the eastern tip of the island where the two rivers become one, a **bench** overlooks the channel and downtown St. Paul. Continue counterclockwise around the island from the confluence point, heading west back toward the footbridge. At the southern

Elm, maple, oak and cottonwood trees line the packed dirt path that loops around Pike Island.

end of the island, you walk along the shore of the Minnesota River; on the northern end, you walk along the Mississippi River. Stay straight ahead at the two trail intersections until you reach the **footbridge.** From here, trace your steps back to the visitors center and parking lot.

Extend the Hike

You can island hop onto Picnic Island for a little more distance and another view of the Minnesota River. Take a left after crossing the Pike Island bridge after finishing the loop and follow the paved path south along the river ,bend to the Picnic Island bridge. Take another left and follow the turf trail loop around the island to get another 2.2 miles in.

Directions

From St. Paul, take MN 5 west for 7 miles. Take the Post Road exit and turn left for 420 feet. Continue on Snelling Lake Road past the park exit for 2.1 miles to the visitors center.

3 WILKIE ROOKERY TRAIL
Minnesota Valley National Wildlife Refuge, Jordan

Distance: 6.1 miles round-trip

Duration: 3.5 hours

Elevation Change: Negligible

Effort: Moderate

Trail: Gravel, packed turf

Users: Hikers, leashed dogs

Season: September-February

Passes/Fees: None

Maps: Maps available on the park website

Contact: Minnesota Valley National Wildlife Refuge, 3815 American Boulevard East, 952/854-5900, www.fws.gov/refuge/minnesota_valley, dawn-dusk daily

---

This trail follows the marshes and lakes that surround Minnesota's largest great blue heron rookery.

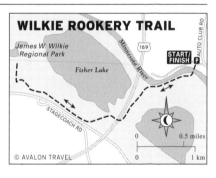

Before you pack your binoculars and bird book, take note that the rookery section of the Wilkie Unit at the Minnesota Valley National Wildlife Refuge is closed March-August each year to accommodate the shy pairs of herons (600 each year) that nest during spring and summer. Trails with viewing areas outside of the rookery remain open all year, however.

Start the Hike

From the Bloomington Ferry parking lot, walk to the pedestrian **footbridge** just a few hundred feet southwest. The bridge crosses the **Minnesota River** toward Rice and Fisher Lakes. The trail is essentially an abandoned road.

One mile from the pedestrian bridge, you come to the boat ramp that provides access to **Rice Lake.** Continue on the trail as it passes under the U.S. Highway 169 freeway bridge. The trail widens to a gravel road here and leads for another 0.9 mile to the **Wilkie parking lot.**

As you head west, you will begin hiking on the **Minnesota River Trail.** At 0.3 mile from the Wilkie parking lot, take a right at the trail intersection to head north toward the river. The trail makes a **1-mile loop,** borders the southern shore of the river, and then heads back south.

Shorten the Hike

Instead of crossing the river from the Bloomington Ferry parking lot, shorten this hike by parking at the Wilkie entrance on the other side of the river. Cross the river on U.S. Highway 169 and exit right to the Wilkie entrance and parking lot. Take a left on the trail that heads northwest toward the river.

Directions

From Minneapolis, head south on I-35 West for 7.2 miles. Take the I-494 West exit for 4.5 miles. Exit onto U.S. Highway 169 South for 3.5 miles. Take the Old Shakopee Road exit and turn left at Riverview Road. Drive 0.7 mile and take a right onto Bloomington Ferry Road. Drive 0.7 mile to Bloomington Ferry Circle and parking lot.

4 LOUISVILLE SWAMP LOOP

Minnesota Valley National Wildlife Refuge, Jordan

Distance: 5.7 miles round-trip

Duration: 3 hours

Elevation Change: 100 feet

Effort: Moderate

Trail: Gravel, mowed grass, packed turf

Users: Hikers, leashed dogs

Season: Year-round

Passes/Fees: None

Maps: Maps available at the trailhead kiosk and the refuge website

Contact: Minnesota Valley National Wildlife Refuge, 3815 American Boulevard East, 952/854-5915, www.fws.gov/refuge/minnesota_valley, dawn-dusk daily

Hike the lush floodplain of the Louisville Swamp.

The Louisville Swamp Loop trail tours bottomlands and forests near the Minnesota River.

Start the Hike

Walk south from the parking lot on the gravel entryway to the grassy trail that starts this hike. The trailhead on the southern end of the parking lot is easy to find. There's a large map and information **kiosk** that gives a brief history of the area. Take a right at the **trail intersection** 0.4 mile from the trailhead. The next mile of trail leads west

LOUISVILLE SWAMP LOOP

145TH ST

START/FINISH P

Minnesota Valley

National

Wildlife Refuge

0   0.5 miles

0   1 km

© AVALON TRAVEL

through the savanna. Two short **spur trails** lead left to the edge of the bluff that overlooks the Louisville Swamp and the creek that runs through it.

At the western end of the trail, take a left at the **intersection** and begin a fairly steep descent through the oak and maple forest to the bottomlands. Follow the **turf trail** across the creek that runs west through the swamp. This can be quite

© JAKE KULJU

Flooded tree stumps and swamp grass fill the Minnesota River Valley at the Louisville Swamps.

difficult during wet seasons and after rains. You will more than likely get your feet wet trying to cross this portion of the trail no matter what time of year it is. Make your way south to **Jabs Farm,** where three original buildings still stand on the 1880 farmstead. Then follow the trail that veers left toward the glacial boulder.

Turn left at the **boulder intersection** to head north for a mile across the swamp and up the ridge to the oak savanna and prairie. Take a right at the **intersection** on top of the ridge to return 0.4 mile to the parking lot and trailhead.

Extend the Hike
After climbing out of the wetland back up to the savanna, take a left instead of heading back to the trailhead and finish out the Little Prairie Loop trail that winds through the tallgrass and wildflower prairie on top of the hill. The loop is nearly 2 miles long and will return you to the trailhead on the western end of the parking lot.

Directions
From Minneapolis, drive south on I-35 West for 7.2 miles. Exit onto I-494 West for 4.5 miles. Take the U.S. Highway 169 South exit and drive south for 16 miles to 145th Street West. Turn right and look for the Louisville Swamp Unit parking lot on your left in 0.5 mile. A park sign is posted at the entrance.

5 BLACK DOG LAKE TRAIL

Minnesota Valley National Wildlife Refuge, Bloomington

Distance: 4 miles round-trip

Duration: 2 hours

Elevation Change: Negligible

Effort: Easy

Trail: Dirt

Users: Hikers, leashed dogs

Season: Year-round

Passes/Fees: None

Maps: Maps available on the park website

Contact: Minnesota Valley National Wildlife Refuge, 3815 American Boulevard East, Bloomington, 952/854-5900, www.fws.gov/refuge/minnesota_valley, dawn-dusk daily

---

Hike near Black Dog Lake's rare calcareous fen habitat.

Calcareous fen is considered the rarest wetland community in the Midwest and one of the rarest in North America. Calcareous fens support unique plant communities with non-acidic peat created by low-oxygen groundwater seepage rich in calcium and other minerals. It is very important to stay on the established trail to maintain the integrity of the fen and its plant community. Some of the plants you may see here include shrubby cinquefoil, sterile sedge, and wild timothy.

Start the Hike

From the parking lot, follow the **dirt path** to the northern edge of the soccer fields through the tree line and across the railroad tracks. The tall, wavy grasses here are examples of what much of this part of the state used to look like. The trail makes a

0.5-mile arc to the northeast and then evens out into a straight line for 1.25 miles as it approaches the **wetland fen** near the lake.

At 0.75 mile from the trailhead, the path threads between an outcropping of Black Dog Lake to the north and a marshy **wetland pond** to the south.

After passing by the pond, the trail veers right to a parking lot on **River Hills Drive.** Turn around here and retrace your steps for 2 miles through the marsh and back through the prairie grasses near the trailhead.

Shorten the Hike

If you have two vehicles in your hiking party, you can turn this into a shuttle hike instead of an "out and back" hike. Park the second car at the River Hills Drive parking lot by taking a left on Cliff Road and another left onto West River Hills Drive for 1.2 miles. The road ends at the gravel parking lot. This cuts the hike in half, turning it into a 2-mile trek from prairie grasses through calcareous fen marshes and wetland ponds.

Directions

From Minneapolis, head south on I-35 West for 12.7 miles. Take exit 4A for Cliff Road and merge onto Cliff Road in 0.3 mile. Continue on River Ridge Boulevard/ Cliff Road West for 0.8 mile. The Cliff Nicollet Park parking lot will be on your left next to the soccer fields.

6 HANREHAN LAKE TRAIL

Murphy-Hanrehan Park Reserve, Lakeville

Distance: 5.1 miles round-trip

Duration: 2.5 hours

Elevation Change: 10 feet

Effort: Easy/moderate

Trail: Packed turf, boardwalk

Users: Hikers, leashed dogs

Season: Year-round

Passes/Fees: None

Maps: Maps available on the park website

Contact: Murphy-Hanrehan Park Reserve, 15501 Murphy Lake Road, Savage, 763/559-9000, www.threeriversparks.org, 5am-10pm daily

Weave your way through the gentle hills that surround Hanrehan Lake.

Murphy-Hanrehan Park Reserve is one of the pockets of woods and water that give southern Minnesota its country feel.

Start the Hike

Begin hiking south from the parking lot. The trail almost immediately **splits,** and you should veer right. The **turf trail** crosses a grassy meadow and then enters the maple and oak woods that arc along the north shore of an approaching pond. The trail continues southeast through the woods, occasionally passing through patches of meadow.

A cross-country ski trail breaks to the right 0.75 mile from the trailhead. Stay to the left to **intersection 10** and take a right to continue through the forest. Stay to the right at the next intersection in 0.3 mile. Over the next 0.5 mile, two more **cross-country ski trails** lead south. Stay eastward at the first, and take a left at the second to head almost straight north for another 0.75 mile. The trail makes a hard turn to the left and in 0.5 mile arcs south along the upper arm of

Hanrehan Lake. When the turf trail doubles back northeast, you will cross a larger section of meadow.

Another cross-country ski trail branches from the trail 0.75 miles from the lake. Keep walking south to **intersection 9** and take a right. Take another right in 0.2 mile to **intersection 3.** Take another right here onto the north-leading **wetland trail.** This 0.75-mile arc passes through the marsh that hugs the eastern shore of Hanrehan Lake. A boardwalk leads through the reeds before the trail enters the higher wooded grounds farther to the south. At **intersection 1,** stay to the right, walking straight west back to the trailhead and parking lot.

Shorten the Hike
You can take a shorter hike that gives you a view of the lake and takes you over the boardwalk by taking a left at intersection 10 and heading north toward Hanrehan Lake. After crossing over the boardwalk and walking along the lake's southern shore, take a right at intersection 1 to return to the trailhead.

Directions
From Minneapolis, head south on I-35 West for 15.2 miles. Take the County Road 42 exit and turn right. Drive for 2 miles and take a left at West Burnsville Parkway; 1.1 miles later, merge onto Hanrehan Lake Boulevard for 1.2 miles. Turn left at Murphy Lake Boulevard. The park entrance is a few hundred feet on your left. The parking lot is to the left.

7 MURPHY LAKE TO MINNREGS LAKE TRAIL

Murphy-Hanrehan Park Reserve, Lakeville

Distance: 6.3 miles round-trip

Duration: 3-3.5 hours

Elevation Change: 100 feet

Effort: Moderate

Trail: Packed turf

Users: Hikers, leashed dogs

Season: Year-round

Passes/Fees: None

Maps: Maps available at the park website

Contact: Murphy-Hanrehan Park Reserve, 15501 Murphy Lake Rd., Savage, 763/559-9000, www.threeriverparks.org, 5am-10pm daily

Trek through wide meadows and thick forests in lake country.

The Murphy Lake trail system passes by the ponds and forests of the park.

Start the Hike

From the parking lot, cross the road and follow the **turf trail** east into the thick woods. You have entered a large **counterclockwise loop** that tours the wooded ponds of the park's central section. On the northern end of the loop, two cross-country ski trails lead north at **intersections 16** and **15**. Stay to the left at all trail intersections until you reach the **parking lot** at the completion of the **2.2-mile loop.**

After returning to the parking lot, walk west on the **unpaved hiking trail** that skirts the northern shore of a **small park pond**. Maple and oak trees provide

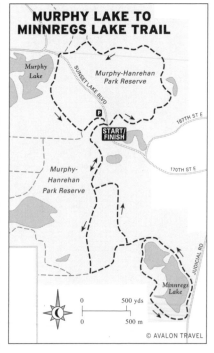

a nice shade canopy for 0.5 mile before the trees give way to prairie. The trail hugs the edge of the grassland at the tree line for another 0.6 mile, and then crosses the **shallow creek** that flows from the park's pond system to the west. At **intersection 40,** take a left. After the creek, the trail reenters the forest and meanders northeast toward **Minnregs Lake.**

Fallen leaves line the path in the early autumn in Murphy-Hanrehan Park Reserve.

The trail splits in 0.25 mile. Take a right to enter the loop that **circles the lake.** The trail soon splits again at the top of the loop. Take a left if you want to take in the sights of the prairie that dominate the eastern side of the water. As the trail leads north again, you will enter a woodland all the way to the top of the loop. If you'd rather finish the loop in the waist-high grass, take a right.

After returning to **intersection 38,** take a right and then another right at **intersection 37** in 0.5 mile. The final stretch leads north to the parking lot through patches of meadow and forest between the scattered ponds that characterize Murphy-Hanrehan Park Reserve.

Shorten the Hike

Getting to Minnregs Lake can take about half the time if you cut out the first loop of the hike. Just head south from the parking lot, take a left at intersection 40, and loop counterclockwise around the lake. At intersection 38, take a right. Take another at intersection 37 and head north back to the trailhead. This shorter hike is 4.1 miles long.

Directions

From Minneapolis, head south on I-35 West for 17 miles. Continue south on I-35 after the merger of I-35 East for another 2 miles. Take the County Road 5 exit and merge onto Kenwood Trail for about 0.5 mile. Turn left at Klamath Trail and drive 0.7 mile to 168th Street West. Take a left for 0.5 mile and continue straight on Judicial Road. Turn right at 170th Street East and continue on Sunset Lake Road for another 0.4 mile. The parking area and trailhead are on the left just before the Equestrian Group Camp.

8 WESTERN LEBANON HILLS HIKING TRAIL

Lebanon Hills Regional Park, Eagan

Distance: 2.5 miles round-trip

Duration: 1.5 hours

Elevation Change: 60 feet

Effort: Easy

Trail: Dirt, packed turf

Users: Hikers, cyclists, leashed dogs

Season: Year-round; cross-country skiing in winter

Passes/Fees: None

Maps: Maps available on the park website

Contact: Lebanon Hills Regional Park, 860 Cliff Road, 651/554-6530, www.co.dakota.mn.us, 5am-10pm daily

Hike through Lebanon Hills Regional Park's western territory.

The western portion of Lebanon Hills Regional Park offers a remote hiking experience.

Start the Hike

From the parking lot, head west along the **packed dirt trail** that leads through the thick pine trees. The pines give way to the maple and oak woods that dominate most of the park. Several mountain-biking paths cross the hiking trail, but don't be tempted to go down them. Most of them are single-lane, one-way bike paths, and bikers can come crashing along with little notice. Stick to the **turf trail** that heads west through the trees. When you reach the spur trail that leads out of the forest to **Galaxie Avenue,** take a left. You will encounter two more hiking **trail intersections.** Stay right at the first and left at the second to remain on the larger trail loop.

When the trail begins to head eastward, it weaves through several very **small ponds.** The trail swings north near the large pond close to Johnny Cake Ridge

Road and passes through the largest of the forest meadows along this hike. The last 0.5 mile of this hike crosses another **mountain-biking trail** and a hiking **trail intersection.** Take a right and follow the turf trail 0.25 mile back to the trailhead and parking lot.

Extend the Hike
Across Johnny Cake Ridge Road, you can follow Sherwood Way above Gerhardt Lake and take a right onto the hiking trail that runs through the forests between Johnny Cake Ridge and Pilot Knob Road. Sherwood Way is just 200 feet south of the parking lot. Walk along the road and follow Sherwood Way to the trailhead on your right. At Pilot Knob, turn around and head back to the parking lot. This will add about 2 miles to your hike.

Directions
From St. Paul, drive 13 miles south on I-35 East. Take the Cliff Road exit, keeping left at the fork to continue toward Cliff Road. Turn left; then take a right at Johnny Cake Ridge Road in 0.7 mile. The parking lot is 0.5 mile ahead on your right, just to the south of a baseball diamond.

© JAKE KULJU

Transitional zones between forest and meadow like this area create a unique habitat for local wildlife.

9 JENSEN LAKE TRAIL
Lebanon Hills Regional Park, Eagan

Distance: 3.3 miles round-trip

Duration: 2 hours

Elevation Change: 60 feet

Effort: Easy

Trail: Dirt, packed turf

Users: Hikers, leashed dogs

Season: Year-round

Passes/Fees: None

Maps: Maps available on the park website

Contact: Lebanon Hills Regional Park, 860 Cliff Road, 651/554-6530, www. co.dakota.mn.us, 5am-10pm daily

---

Walk along Bridge Pond and the forests that surround Jensen Lake.

This peaceful hike is a walk in the woods.

Start the Hike
From the picnic shelter, head southeast on the **packed-dirt trail** that leads through the meadow to the lake. Take a right at the trail intersection to start a **counterclockwise loop** around the water. The trail almost immediately delves into the woods.

As the path turns to the east, it follows the lakeshore closely, not leaving it until the far eastern edge of the water. A midsize peninsula juts into the lake near the small island in its eastern arm. At **intersection 10,** between the lake and a park pond, take a right to move toward **Bridge Pond.** When you get to the water, you'll cross the pond's namesake bridge. The trail passes through an open meadow briefly before reaching the footbridge. On the other side, it goes back into the woods.

The trail splits north and south after the bridge. Take a left to head north along the **eastern edge of the pond.** As you head north, the trail crosses a wider **horse**

© JAKE KULJU

an open meadow along the Jensen Lake Trail

trail. Keep north for another 0.25 mile to **intersection 15.** Take a left here and recross the horse trail in another 0.15 mile. The next 0.2 mile is through a larger meadow, with scattered trees. Take a left at **intersection 9** and a right at the next trail intersection 0.1 mile later. This is the final 0.75 mile of the hike along **Jensen Lake's north shore.** When you reach the meadow opening along the shoreline, take a right to return to the trailhead and parking lot near the picnic shelter.

Shorten the Hike
Shorten this hike by forgoing the Bridge Pond section of the hike. Just take left turns at intersections 10 and 8 to make one 2.2-mile loop around Jensen Lake.

Directions
From St. Paul, drive 9.6 miles south on I-35 East. Take the Pilot Knob Road exit and turn right. Drive for 3.5 miles to Carriage Hills Drive. Take a left and an immediate right onto Coach Road. Coach Road is a large parking loop. The picnic shelter and trailhead are east of the parking lot.

10 HOLLAND AND O'BRIEN LAKES TRAIL

Lebanon Hills Regional Park, Eagan

🦌 🌼 👫

Distance: 4.6 miles round-trip

Duration: 3 hours

Elevation Change: 70 feet

Effort: Moderate

Trail: Packed turf, dirt

Users: Hikers

Season: Year-round

Passes/Fees: None

Maps: Maps available on the park website

Contact: Lebanon Hills Regional Park, 860 Cliff Road, 651/554-6530, www.co.dakota.mn.us, 5am-10pm daily

Explore the lakes of Lebanon Hills Regional Park.

The beautiful landscape and rolling hills of Lebanon Hills Regional Park make for excellent hiking.

HOLLAND AND O'BRIEN LAKES TRAIL

Start the Hike

Start from the **Holland Lake trailhead** and walk south toward the water. The turf trail cuts west and then arcs to the south between the lake and a smaller pond. Take a right at **intersection 19** for 0.2 mile to **intersection 16.** Take a left here for 0.25 mile to **intersection 25** and then turn right. At **intersection 29,** take another right and cross the wider horse trail that passes through the center of the park. The terrain here switches from thick woods to scattered trees and meadows.

Continue south for 0.1 mile to **intersection 24** and take a right. **Intersection 15** lies 0.25 mile ahead through the thick hardwood forest. Take a left here and walk south to **Bridge Pond** for 0.5 mile. You will cross another horse trail at

Indian Paintbrush and Butterfly Weed flowers bloom amidst the prairie grass.

intersection 18 and a hiking trail near the bridge. Stay to your left on the eastern side of the pond and follow the trail south to **intersections 22** and **23** between **Bridge** and **Lily Ponds.** Stay to the right on the forest turf trail. The wider horse trail isn't the way you want to go.

For the next 0.7 mile, the trail leads northeast near the south shore of **O'Brien Lake.** More thick woods line the path. At **intersection 35,** take a right to continue heading northeast near the south shore of the much smaller **Portage Lake.** Take a left at **intersection 49** after crossing a horse trail, and a right just 0.1 mile later at **intersection 45.** There is a bit of a hill here as you head north toward Schulze Lake. Walk 0.2 mile up the trail to **intersection 53** and take a left. Take a left at **intersection 46** and walk along the western tip of **Schulze Lake** to **intersection 43.** Take a right and head north to **intersection 47.** Stay to the right here as well, continuing north on the western shore of the lake to **intersection 50.** Take a left here and walk 0.2 mile to **intersection 40.** The trail finally breaks into the grasslands between **McDonough** and **Schulze Lakes.** Take another right and follow the winding forest and meadow trail for 0.8 mile to **intersection 32.** Take a right here through more meadow and forest mixed landscape to **intersection 29.** Take a right and another right at **intersection 25** along the western shore of **Holland Lake.** At **intersection 19,** take a right to head 0.25 mile back to the trailhead and parking lot.

Shorten the Hike

Instead of arcing east all the way to Schulze Lake, you can make a shorter loop around O'Brien and Cattail Lakes. Take left turns at intersections 35 and 33, and a right at intersection 24 to head back north along the trail that leads from the parking lot.

Directions

From St. Paul, drive south on I-35 East for 9.6 miles. Take the Pilot Knob Road exit and turn right onto Pilot Knob for 2.8 miles. Turn left at Cliff Road for 1 mile and take a right onto Lexington Avenue South. Park in the parking loop at the end of the road.

11 COTTONWOOD RIVER AND HIKING CLUB TRAIL

Flandrau State Park, New Ulm

Distance: 5.6 miles round-trip

Duration: 3 hours

Elevation Change: 210 feet

Effort: Moderate/strenuous

Trail: Dirt, packed turf

Users: Hikers, leashed dogs

Season: Year-round

Passes/Fees: $5 daily vehicle permit fee

Maps: Maps available at the park office and on the park website

Contact: Flandrau State Park, 1300 Summit Avenue, 507/233-9800, www.dnr.state.mn.us, 8am-10pm daily

---

Visit the sand-bottom swimming pond, oxbow marshes, and oak grove bluffs along the Cottonwood River.

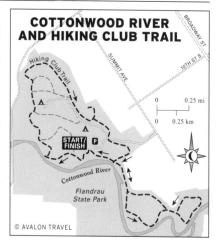

The trail system here ranges from bottomland forest loops to bluff-top overlooks, and the park is just a hop, skip, and a jump away from New Ulm.

Start the Hike

From the parking lot, walk west away from the park road to the **beach house shelter.** Just south of here is the sand-bottom pond **swimming area.** Take a right at the beach house to begin on the **Hiking Club trail.** Once upon a time, tallgrass prairie covered this entire region.

You will come to a short spur trail 0.3 mile from the parking lot that leads to the first **overlook point.** Take a left onto the trail and take a moment to look over the Cottonwood River. Return to the trail and take a left. Keep left at the **trail intersection** 0.2 mile up the trail, staying on the Hiking Club path. As the trail

Driftwood and fallen logs are left behind from a recent flood.

leads north, it slowly climbs up the valley away from the river; 0.5 mile from the overlook point, the trail passes by a walk-in **campsite** and crosses a **gravel park road** and parking lot into an open grassland. Grasshoppers and butterflies flit between the Indian paintbrush and blazing star.

Continue north, following the **Hiking Club trail signs;** 0.3 mile from the park road, the trail arcs east along the ridgeline that forms the boundary of the park. The trail follows the ridge for 0.9 mile to the **Indian Point spur trail.** Take a left here and climb 110 feet up the ridge. Take a left on the **Ridge Trail** to the overlook point. This sweeping view covers the entire park and river as it winds its way southeast.

Return to the **Hiking Club trail** and take a left past the trailer sanitation station. At 0.3 mile from the Indian Point trail, the Hiking Club trail crosses two **park road intersections.** Follow the trail southeast, keeping on the Hiking Club trail, which is marked with signs. In 0.3 mile, take a left up the steps to climb a ridge up to another overlook point. Continue south from the overlook on the **River Trail** on the **Old Island Loop.** Take a right 0.6 mile from the last intersection to yet another overlook point. Take another right onto the **River Loop,** which passes by the **dam site** that once blocked the Cottonwood River. From the dam, finish the loop back to the overlook point and retrace your steps for 0.1 mile. Take a right at the intersection on the north end of the **Old Island Loop** and follow the ridgeline back to the **Hiking Club trail.** Take a left down the steps and another left to head west on the Hiking Club trail back to the beach house and parking lot.

Shorten the Hike

If climbing isn't your strong suit, you can forgo the 100-foot climb to Indian Point overlook. Just keep to the right when you come to the spur trail that leads up the hill. This will shave 0.4 mile off your hike and keep you in the bottomlands formed by the Cottonwood River.

Directions

From Minneapolis, drive south on I-35 West for 7 miles. Take the I-494 West exit. In 4.5 miles, exit onto U.S. Highway 169 South. Drive 65 miles and merge onto

U.S. Highway 14 West for another 24 miles. Turn left at 20th Street South into New Ulm and take a right onto MN 15 in 1.1 miles. In 1 mile, turn left at 10th Street South, then left at Summit Avenue. Take a right into the park entrance. The office is 0.3 mile ahead. Follow signs to the parking lot 0.2 mile ahead. Park in the southern lot near the beach.

12 SEPPMAN WINDMILL TRAIL

Minneopa State Park, Mankato

Best: Wildflowers

Distance: 4 miles round-trip

Duration: 2 hours

Elevation Change: 50 feet

Effort: Easy

Trail: Packed turf

Users: Hikers, leashed dogs

Season: Year-round; snowshoeing in winter

Passes/Fees: $5 daily vehicle permit fee

Maps: Maps available at the information office and on the park website

Contact: Minneopa State Park, 54497 Gadwall Road, 507/389-5464, www.dnr.state.mn.us, 8am-10pm daily

---

See the stone gristmill, Seppman Windmill, and the grasslands that surround the Minnesota River in Minneopa State Park.

This Minnesota River Valley hike is a haven of native landscapes.

Start the Hike

Start by walking south from the parking loop toward the picnic area on the **Hiking Club trail.** Follow the trail as it swings northwest past the park office and crosses the **park road.**

Continue west on the Hiking Club trail; 1.3 miles from the trailhead, take a left at the prairie spur trail that leads to the **Seppman Windmill.** From the windmill, return to the **main trail** and take a left to continue touring the park's grassland and oak savanna. The trail crosses the **park road** just after the windmill intersection. Stay on the Hiking Club trail as it swings southeast toward the **campground.**

After crossing the **park road** once more, take a left off the Hiking Club trail on the **spur trail** that leads northeast along Minneopa Creek to its confluence point

© JAKE KULJU

A dragonfly rests on the undergrowth in Minneopa State Park.

with the Minnesota River. The trail crosses some railroad tracks through the forest near the river and passes an **overlook point.** Return to the Hiking Club trail and take a left to return to the parking loop, just a few hundred feet to the south.

Extend the Hike

This park was originally created to preserve the waterfall on the Minneopa Creek in the southern portion of the park. You can drive south from the parking lot across MN 68 and 69 to the parking lot at the head of the falls. A small trail loops around the area. Limestone steps lead down to the cascade, and the turf trail climbs the wooded hills across the creek to give a view of the bottomlands from above. This adds 0.4 mile to your hike and gives you a beautiful waterfall view.

Directions

From Minneapolis, head south on I-35 West for 7.2 miles. Take the I-494 West exit. Exit onto U.S. Highway 169 South in 4.5 miles; 70 miles later, turn right at MN 68 past Mankato. Drive 1.6 miles and turn right at Minneopa State Park Road. After the information office, take a right into the parking lot and trailhead.

BIG WOODS LOOP TO TIMBER DOODLE TRAIL

Sakatah Lake State Park, Waterville

Best: Wildflowers

Distance: 6.1 miles round-trip

Duration: 3-3.5 hours

Elevation Change: 270 feet

Effort: Moderate/strenuous

Trail: Packed turf, gravel road

Users: Hikers, leashed dogs

Season: Year-round

Passes/Fees: $5 daily vehicle permit fee

Maps: Maps available at the park office and on the park website

Contact: Sakatah Lake State Park, 50499 Sakatah Lake State Park Road, 507/362-4438, www.dnr.state.mn.us, open 24/7

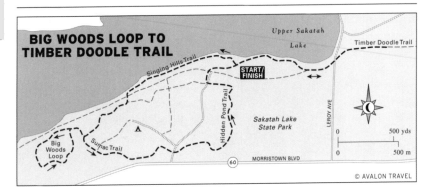

Climb the hills that roll south from the southern shores of Upper Sakatah Lake.

This forested trail passes through beautiful rolling hills.

Start the Hike

From the parking lot, head north for a few hundred feet on the turf trail that leads

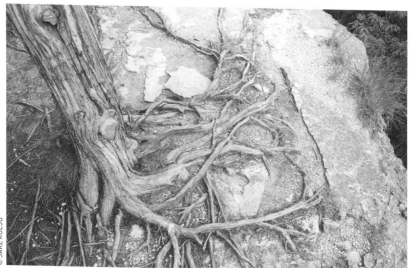

© JAKE KULJU

The roots of a cedar tree search for footholds along a rock surface in Sakatah Lake State Park.

downhill to the lake. Take a left and follow the lakeshore west for 0.6 mile to the paved **Singing Hills Trail.** Walk up the hillside and cross the trail, taking a right at the turf **trail intersection.**

The trail enters the **Big Woods Loop** 0.4 mile from the paved trail crossing, climbing the undulating hills that characterize this portion of the state. You walk up 100 feet of hillside through this thick basswood, oak, and maple jungle and walk right back down it on this **0.6-mile loop.**

After leaving the loop, take a right to continue a gradual uphill climb along the **Sumac Trail.** Stay to the right at the next two trail intersections, crossing the park road near the park office onto the **Hidden Pond Trail.** The trail crosses it again 1 mile from the park road, this time heading west. Take a right at the road and follow it north for just a few hundred feet to the picnic area parking lot. Retrace your steps downhill to the lake and take a right this time, past the fishing pier toward the boat access ramp. Continue east past the **group campsite** on the **Timber Doodle Trail.** Take a right on the loop at the end of the trail and retrace your steps heading west to the parking lot and trailhead.

Shorten the Hike

Remain in the hills and shorten this hike by 2.1 miles by not taking the Timber Doodle branch of the trail. After making the Big Woods Loop and returning to the parking lot, find the trailhead and call it a day after 4 miles of hiking through rolling hills and thick maple and oak forest.

Directions

From Minneapolis, drive south on I-35 West for 16.6 miles. Continue south for another 31 miles after the I-35 East merger in Burnsville. Take the MN 60 exit and merge onto 30th Avenue NW in Faribault. Drive 12.8 miles to the Sakatah Lake State Park entrance on your right. Follow signs to the picnic area and fishing pier parking lot.

14 HIDDEN FALLS TO HOPE TRAIL LOOP

Nerstrand-Big Woods State Park, Nerstrand

Best: Waterfalls, Wildflowers

Distance: 4.7 miles round-trip

Duration: 2.5 hours

Elevation Change: 90 feet

Effort: Easy/moderate

Trail: Packed dirt

Users: Hikers, leashed dogs

Season: Year-round

Passes/Fees: $5 daily vehicle permit fee

Maps: Maps available at the park office and on the park website

Contact: Nerstrand-Big Woods State Park, 9700 170th Street East, 507/333-4840, www.dnr.state.mn.us, 8am-10pm daily

---

View the hidden falls of Prairie Creek.

This park's trails are beautiful places to enjoy nature any time of year.

HIDDEN FALLS TO HOPE TRAIL LOOP

© AVALON TRAVEL

Start the Hike

From the southeastern corner of the parking lot, follow the trail east for 0.1 mile; then take a left toward the **picnic area** (restrooms and drinking fountain available). The trail arcs northeast for 0.5 mile through the woods to **Hidden Falls.** Take a left at the falls across **Prairie Creek**, and then turn right about 100 feet after the bridge, continuing north on the **Fawn Trail.** Follow this 1-mile arc into the northernmost region of the park.

Take a right on the **Hope Trail,** near a large open meadow in the middle of the woods. Walk northwest for 0.2 mile and take a right on the **Hope Trail Loop.** This

a look up the creek above Hidden Falls

1.2-mile loop leads through more thick woods and skirts the edge of another open meadow before swinging south and east. Retrace your steps on the Hope Trail for 0.2 mile and then take a right to finish the **Fawn Trail.** Take a right onto the **Beaver Trail,** which leads to the creek. You cut west here and meander through more woods and hills to a trail intersection 0.6 mile ahead. Take a right and cross the oak **footbridge** at Prairie Creek. Continue for 0.2 mile and take a left, then another left 0.1 mile later. This path leads around the walk-in **campsites** into a thick stand of white oaks. Take a left at the trail intersection. The parking lot and trailhead are 0.3 mile ahead.

Shorten the Hike

If you'd like to enjoy the view of hidden falls without the full 4.7-mile hike, you can take a shorter 1.5-mile jaunt to the creek and back to the trailhead. After reaching the falls, turn around and follow your steps back to the parking lot or take a left at the first intersection south of the falls. This path arcs south around the trail maintenance station and emerges back on the park road that leads to the campground. Cross the road and take a right. The trail back to the parking lot leads to your left just a few hundred feet to the east.

Directions

From Minneapolis, drive south on I-35 West for 16.6 miles. Continue south for another 28.8 miles after the I-35 East merger in Burnsville. Take exit 59 toward Faribault and merge onto MN 21 for 1 mile. Turn left at 20th Street NW and drive for 1 mile. Turn right at 2nd Avenue NW and left at 14th Street NW. In 1.4 miles, turn left at 14th Street NE for 0.5 mile. Continue on Cagger Trail for 1.4 miles. Turn left at Cannon City Boulevard and drive for 0.8 mile. Turn right onto Cannon City Path and continue on Nerstrand Boulevard for 3.3 miles. Turn left at Hall Avenue for 1 mile and turn right at 170th Street East for 1.5 miles. The park entrance is on the left. Take a left after the visitors center into the parking lot.

15 RICE LAKE TRAIL

Rice Lake State Park, Owatonna

Distance: 3.5 miles round-trip

Duration: 1.75 hours

Elevation Change: Negligible

Effort: Easy

Trail: Packed turf, gravel road

Users: Hikers, leashed dogs

Season: Year-round

Passes/Fees: $5 daily vehicle permit fee

Maps: Maps available at the park office and on the park website

Contact: Rice Lake State Park, 8485 Rose Street, 507/455-5871, www.dnr.state.mn.us, 8am-10pm daily

Explore the transition zones between hardwood forest, marshy wetland, lakes, and prairie.

The Rice Lake area is notable for its diversity of habitat. Marshes, lakes, meadows, and woods are all found here and attract a significant amount of wildlife.

Start the Hike

From the north end of the parking lot, follow the turf trail to the right toward the **wooden trail shelter.** Continue following the trail north as it breaks out of the trees and makes a 0.6-mile arc to the west, parallel to MN 19. Just before the trail crosses the **park road,** it enters the maple, oak, and aspen forest that characterizes most of the park. Cross the road and walk south for 0.5 mile to the **boat access road.** The trail leaves the trees once more and passes through the wide prairie meadow.

Take a right on the **gravel road** to the boat access ramp and another right on the **turf trail** that leads north where it crosses the road. The trail makes a **0.9-mile loop** through the woods and along the marshy shore of the lake.

The reedy shores of Rice Lake are a haven for wildlife and waterfowl.

After finishing the loop, return to the boat access ramp and follow the trail as it crosses the **park road.** The next mile of trail closely follows the lakeshore. As the trail bends away from the lake, it returns to the wooden shelter. Take a left here and return to the parking lot, just 0.2 mile to the west.

Extend the Hike

If you'd rather not walk along the park road, you can take a right at the first trail intersection and follow in the inner curve of Rice Lake to the loop at the end of the trail, then turn around and follow your steps back to the trailhead and parking lot. This will add 0.1 mile to your trip and keep you closer to the marshy shores of the lake throughout the hike.

Directions

From St. Paul, drive south on I-35 East for 19.2 miles. Continue on I-35 South after the merger of I-35 West in Burnsville for another 45.4 miles. Take exit 42A for Owatonna. Merge onto Hoffman Drive and drive for 1.2 miles. Turn left at MN 19 and drive for 6.4 miles. Veer right to stay on MN 19 for 2.2 miles to the park entrance. Turn right into the park. Turn left after the park office for 0.3 mile and make another left after 0.3 mile, following signs to the walk-in campsite parking lot.

ZUMBRO RIVER AND HIGH MEADOW TRAIL

Oxbow Park, Rochester

Distance: 5.1 miles round-trip

Duration: 2.75 hours

Elevation Change: 120 feet

Effort: Moderate

Trail: Packed dirt

Users: Hikers, leashed dogs

Season: Year-round

Passes/Fees: None

Maps: Maps available on the park website

Contact: Oxbow Park, 5731 County Road 105 NW, Byron, 507/775-2451, www. co.olmsted.mn.us, 5am-10pm daily

Take a walk along the winding ox-bows of the Zumbro River and the prairie meadows that rise above.

Tucked into the ridge that borders the large bend of the Zumbro River, Oxbow Park is a beautifully preserved area full of hardwood forests and riverside trails.

Start the Trail

From the parking lot and picnic area, cross the first bridge and take a right onto the **Zumbro Trail.** The trailhead is located in the middle of the oxbow that the park derives its name from. The river nearly doubles back on it-self, almost forming a circle as it winds northward along the ridgeline. Follow the Zumbro Trail for 1.5 miles as it fol-lows the curve of the river. When the

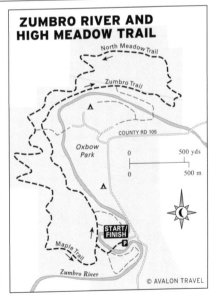

Zumbro Trail splits on the north bank of the river, take a left and follow the **North Meadow Trail** as it climbs the ridge up to the patch of prairie on top of the bluff.

A trail cuts through the diameter of the **North Meadow Loop.** Stay to the right at both of its intersection points to stay on the tree-line trail that borders the meadow.

The trail swings south and follows the eastern shore of the **Zumbro River,** though this time from up above. The trail dips into a small valley but soon climbs back up along the **Maple Trail.**

The Maple Trail leads for 1.5 miles south, twisting through the forest and eventually descending to the bottomlands near the first bridge. Take a right at the **Zumbro Trail** intersection and a left to cross the bridge back to the picnic area and parking lot at the trailhead.

Extend the Hike

You can add 0.5 mile to this hike and see some different terrain by taking a left after crossing the bridge from the oxbow parking lot. This loop is called the River Loop and leads you through the sumac and meadow grasses that line the bottomlands near the river. As you finish the loop and continue north on the Zumbro Trail, watch how the plants and trees thicken into a forest.

Directions

From St. Paul, drive east on I-94 for 1.3 miles. Take the U.S. Highway 52 South exit. Drive 59 miles to Pine Island. Take a right on Main Street and head south for 1.4 miles. Turn right at 8th Street SW and left at County Road 3. In 0.6 mile, turn right at County Road 5. Drive for 9.8 miles to Valleyhigh Road NW. Turn left at County Road 105 for 0.5 mile. Turn left at Oxbow Park Drive into the picnic area parking lot. Restrooms and drinking water are available in the Oxbow parking lot, as well as in the picnic area near the campground.

NORTH TRAIL, PRAIRIE RIDGE TRAIL, AND THE DAM OVERLOOK

Chester Woods Park, Rochester

Distance: 5.6 miles round-trip

Duration: 3 hours

Elevation Change: 100 feet

Effort: Moderate

Trail: Packed dirt

Users: Hikers, horse riders, leashed dogs

Season: Year-round; parts of trail used for cross-country skiing in winter

Passes/Fees: $5 daily vehicle permit fee

Maps: Maps available on the park website

Contact: Chester Woods Park, 8378 U.S. Highway 14 East, Eyota, 507/285-7050, www.co.olmsted.mn.us/parks, 5am-10pm daily

This loop climbs through thick woods and open meadows on the rugged bluffs north of Bear Creek and its headwaters.

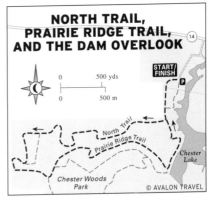

Chester Woods Park is a collection of fields, oak woods, and bluff prairie lands that surround Chester Lake.

Start the Hike

From the parking lot, follow the **North Trail** as it leads west and then juts sharply south along the park border. At the **Prairie Ridge Trail** intersection, take a right to continue on the **North Trail.** Keep to the right at all trail intersections for the next 2 miles. The wide dirt trail borders a thick stand of trees for about 0.2 mile and then breaks into open prairie again.

At the **third trail intersection,** stay to the right and follow the path as it curves to the south through the oak forest. Take another right and then a left to join the **Prairie Ridge Trail.** It's helpful to have a map, as the trail intersections get tricky

a view over the tree canopy above Bear Creek in Chester Woods Park

over the next mile. The Prairie Ridge Trail leads straight east for 0.25 mile before turning south toward **Bear Creek.** Take a left at the creek and continue on the Prairie Ridge Trail as it angles northeast on the ridge above the waterway. Stay to the left at the next trail intersection and to the right at the following two. The wide dirt path is shared by riders on horseback; be sure to give them right of way.

At the **Dam Overlook Trail** intersection, take a right and walk 0.2 mile to the dam overlook area. Continue north on the Dam Overlook Trail loop and take a right at the next intersection. This path leads to one of the park's gravel roads. Take a left for 0.1 mile to the horse trailer parking area and trailhead.

Hike Nearby

You can cross Bear Creek on the western end of the park by taking a right at the bridge that leads south from the Prairie Ridge Trail. Cross the bridge and take a left, following the South Sand Prairie Trail east to another creek crossing. Take a right after crossing back to the north of the creek to the dam overlook. From here, follow the Dam Overlook Trail north back to the horse trailer parking lot.

Directions

From St. Paul, drive east on I-94 for 1.3 miles. Take the U.S. Highway 52 South exit. Drive for 76.8 miles and take the U.S. Highway 14 East exit. Merge onto U.S. Highway 14 and drive for 8.7 miles to the park entrance on your right. Take your first right and then a left, following signs to the horse trailer parking lot. Restrooms are available at the park information office.

18 SUGAR CAMP HOLLOW AND BIG SPRING TRAIL

Forestville/Mystery Cave State Park, Preston

Best: Historical Hikes

Distance: 11.8 miles round-trip

Duration: 7-8 hours

Elevation Change: 520 feet

Effort: Strenuous

Trail: Packed turf

Users: Hikers, leashed dogs

Season: Year-round

Passes/Fees: $5 daily vehicle permit fee

Maps: Maps available at the park office and on the park website

Contact: Forestville/Mystery Cave State Park, 21071 County Road 118, 507/937-3251, www.dnr.state.mn.us, 8am-10pm daily

Discover a natural spring, a hilltop cemetery, and an abandoned 19th-century town on this hike.

This hike through Forestville/Mystery Cave State Park is full of history.

Start the Hike

From the parking lot, take a right onto the turf trail that follows the creek. The trail borders the northern edge of historic **Forestville** before crossing the park road. Take a left onto the trail across the road and follow it north to the **River Bottom Trail.** Half a mile from the park road, the trail cuts northwest toward the old **1880 high school** and **brickyard sites.** Another 0.5 mile from the trail curve and just past the brickyard is a hitching rail at the bottom of the **Zumbro Hill Cemetery Trail.** Make the 180-foot climb to the top of the hill.

Crash back down the hill to the hitching post and take a right on the **Sugar Camp Hollow Trail.** This trail leads through more thick forest and the undulating hills that roll through the area. Choose the middle path at the trail intersection 0.8 mile from the hitching post and continue south on the **Oak Ridge Trail.** The trail goes quickly downhill toward **Forestville Creek and** then splits. Take the right fork and cross the creek, then take another right on the trail that parallels

SUGAR CAMP HOLLOW AND BIG SPRING TRAIL

★ ZUMBRO HILL CEMETERY

Sugar Camp Hollow Trail

River Bottom Trail

Oak Ridge Trail

Forestville/
Mystery Cave
State Park

P

START/
FINISH

301

Maple
Ridge
Trail

Big Spring Trail

301

BIG SPRING ★

© AVALON TRAVEL

0   0.5 miles

0   1 km

the park road; 0.5 mile from the creek, the trail crosses the park road and leads south past the park office on the **Maple Ridge Trail** for 0.75 mile to the Angler's Parking Lot. Cross the road and follow the trail south back through the group camp down the hill as the trail arcs east. Take a right at the next trail intersection and cross the **South Branch Root River,** then take another right on the **Big Spring Trail.** The path continues through the thick woods, with occasional openings of meadow.

The Big Spring Trail follows **Canfield Creek** to its source at Big Spring. This **2.8-mile trek** through the creek valley forest is worth it to see the gushing waters at **Big Spring.** Turn around and follow the trail back north, cross the river, and take a right. This trail leads north along the park road and crosses at the parking lot for anglers. Take a right at the parking lot past the amphitheater and up the hill past the trailer sanitation station. The path crosses the road again and arcs northward along the river and crosses the park road once more. Take a right on the other side of the road and walk 0.2 mile back to the parking lot and trailhead.

Shorten the Hike

You don't have to bust your butt through almost 12 miles of trails to get the essence of Forestville/Mystery Cave State Park. From the parking lot, you can head north and follow the River Bottom Trail to the Zumbro Hill Cemetery spur trail, then link onto the Sugar Camp Hollow Trail heading west. This shortens the hike by more than 7 miles, still giving you a 4-mile uphill workout through the woods.

Directions

From St. Paul, head east on I-94 for 1.3 miles. Take the U.S. Highway 52 South exit. Drive for 108.8 miles to MN 16. Take a left and drive for 3.1 miles. Turn

© JAKE KULJU

a whitetail deer track sunk deep in the mud

left at County Road 11. Drive for 1.2 miles and turn right at County Road 118, which leads into the park. In 3.8 miles, turn right at County Road 12 and park in the Root River parking lot.

19 BIG ISLAND TO GREAT MARSH TRAIL

Myre-Big Island State Park, Albert Lea

Distance: 6 miles round-trip

Duration: 3 hours

Elevation Change: Negligible

Effort: Easy/moderate

Trail: Packed turf, dirt

Users: Hikers, leashed dogs

Season: Year-round

Passes/Fees: $5 resident vehicle permit fee ($10 nonresidents)

Maps: Maps available at the park office and nature center

Contact: Myre-Big Island State Park, 19499 780th Avenue, 507/379-3403, www.dnr.state.mn.us

---

Loop around Big Island and the wetland plains of the Great Marsh on the north shore of Albert Lea Lake.

The wetland marshes, oak savanna, and maple and basswood forests along this trail system are one of Minnesota's finest natural outlets.

Start the Hike

From the parking lot, take a right on the **Big Island Trail,** which circles the island. Before you finish the **1.1-mile loop** around the island, take a left before crossing the park road. This path leads to the mainland and the wide prairie that leads to the Great Marsh. Take a left at the next trail intersection 0.3 mile from Big Island and follow the north shore of **Albert Lea Lake.** A stand of trees hugs the water here before opening to more prairie and wetland. Half a mile from the intersection, the trail crosses the park road into the **Great Marsh;** 0.25 mile from the road, the trail passes by a parking lot. Take a right at the parking lot and head north on the **Great Marsh Trail.**

Take a right 0.3 mile north of the parking lot through the wetland and prairie, then turn left on the **Blazing Star State Trail.** Follow this wide path west for 0.5 mile, then take a left at the **Great Marsh Trail** intersection. Walk south through the marsh for 0.3 mile before taking another right onto the interpretive portion of the Great Marsh Trail. Signs and kiosks with photos and information about the marsh habitat and the creatures that dwell here show up intermittently along

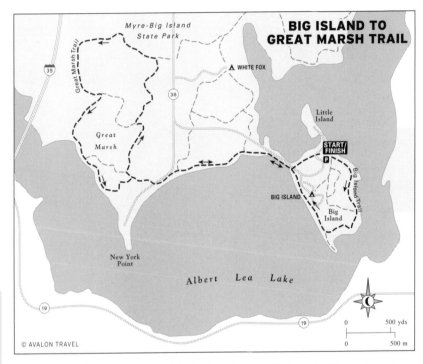

the trail, as well as information kiosks that give insight into the Native American history of the area. When you return to the marsh parking lot, cross the road and retrace your steps to Big Island. Back on the island, take a left and walk for 0.2 mile back to the picnic area and trailhead parking lot.

Shorten the Hike

For a much shorter hike that stays in the trees, just make the 1.5-mile loop around Big Island. Or, if you are more interested in the Great Marsh than the wooded island, park in the Great Marsh Trail parking lot on the way to the group center and make the Great Marsh loop. This will make a 4.5-mile hike through the wetland plain and keep you on the mainland.

Directions

From St. Paul, drive south on I-35 East for 19.2 miles. Continue on I-35 South for 76.1 miles after the merger of I-35 West in Burnsville. Take the County Highway 46 East exit and turn left at MN 116. Turn right at 780th Avenue in Albert Lea. Drive for 2 miles to the park entrance and take your second left. On Big Island, take a left, following signs to the picnic area parking lot. Restrooms and a drinking fountain are available in the nature center by the parking lot.

RESOURCES

PARK INFORMATION SOURCES
Minnesota State Parks
For more information on these state parks, visit www.dnr.state.mn.us.

Afton State Park
6959 Peller Avenue South
Hastings, MN 55033
651/436-5391

Banning State Park
P.O. Box 643
Sandstone, MN 55072
320/245-2668

Carley State Park
c/o Whitewater State Park
Box 256, Route 1
Altura, MN 55910
507/932-3007

Charles A. Lindbergh State Park
1615 Lindbergh Drive South
Little Falls, MN 56345
320/616-2525

Crow Wing State Park
3124 State Park Road
Brainerd, MN 56401
218/825-3075

Father Hennepin State Park
41294 Father Hennepin Park Road
Isle, MN 56342
320/676-8763

Flandrau State Park
1300 Summit Avenue
New Ulm, MN 56073
507/233-9800

Forestville/Mystery Cave State Park
21071 County Road 118
Preston, MN 55965
507/352-5111

Fort Snelling State Park
101 Snelling Lake Road
St. Paul, MN 55111
612/725-2389

Frontenac State Park
29223 County 28 Boulevard
Frontenac, MN 55026
651/345-3401

Great River Bluffs State Park
43605 Kipp Drive
Winona, MN 55987
507/643-6849

Interstate State Park
P.O. Box 254
Taylors Falls, MN 55084
651/465-5711

Jay Cooke State Park
780 MN 210
Carlton, MN 55718
218/384-4610

Lake Maria State Park
11411 Clementa Avenue NW
Monticello, MN 55362
763/878-2325

Mille Lacs Kathio State Park
15066 Kathio State Park Road
Onamia, MN 56359
320/532-3523

Minneopa State Park
54497 Gadwall Road
Mankato, MN 56001
507/389-5464

Minnesota Valley State Park
19825 Park Boulevard
Jordan, MN 55352
952/492-6400

Moose Lake State Park
4252 County Road 137
Moose Lake, MN 55767
218/485-5420

Myre-Big Island State Park
19499 780th Avenue
Albert Lea, MN 56007
507/379-3403

Nerstrand-Big Woods State Park
9700 170th Street East
Nerstrand, MN 55053
507/333-4840

Rice Lake State Park
8485 Rose Street
Owatonna, MN 55060
507/455-5871

Sakatah Lake State Park
50499 Sakatah Lake State Park Road
Waterville, MN 56096
507/362-4438

Sibley State Park
800 Sibley Park Road NE
New London, MN 56273
320/354-2055

St. Croix State Park
30065 St. Croix Park Road
Hinckley, MN 55037
320/384-6591

Whitewater State Park
Box 256, Route 1
Altura, MN 55910
507/932-3007

Wild River State Park
39797 Park Trail
Center City, MN 55012
651/583-2125

William O'Brien State Park
16821 O'Brien Trail North
Marine on St. Croix, MN 55047
651/433-0500

National Wildlife Refuges
For more information on these refuges, visit www.fws.gov/refuges.

Minnesota Valley National Wildlife Refuge
3815 American Boulevard East
Bloomington, MN 55425
952/854-5900

Rice Lake National Wildlife Refuge
36298 MN 65
McGregor, MN 55760
218/768-2402

Wisconsin State Parks
101 South Webster Street
P.O. Box 7921
Madison, WI 53707
608/266-2621
www.dnr.wi.gov/topic/parks/

County Parks

State parks don't have all the best trails! These county parks provide beautiful natural settings full of wildlife, wildflowers, and wilderness.

Anoka County Parks
550 Bunker Lane Boulevard NW
Andover, MN 55304
763/767-2820
www.anokacountyparks.com

Carver County Parks
11360 U.S. Highway 212 West, Suite 2
Cologne, MN 55322
952/466-5250
www.co.carver.mn.us

Dakota County Parks
14955 Galaxie Avenue
Apple Valley, MN 55124
952/891-7000
www.co.dakota.mn.us

Ramsey County Parks
5287 Otter Lake Road
White Bear Township, MN 55110
651/748-2500
www.co.ramsey.mn.us/parks

Three Rivers Park District
3000 Xenium Lane North
Plymouth, MN 55441
763/559-9000
www.threeriversparks.org

Washington County Parks
11660 Myeron Road North
Stillwater, MN 55082
651/430-4300
www.co.washington.mn.us

Wright County Parks
1901 MN 25 North
Buffalo, MN 55313
763/682-7693
www.co.wright.mn.us

City Parks

City of Roseville Parks & Recreation
2660 Civic Center Drive
Roseville, MN 55113
651/792-7006
www.ci.roseville.mn.us

Minneapolis Park & Recreation Board
2117 West River Road
Minneapolis, MN 55411
612/230-6400
www.minneapolisparks.org

St. Paul Parks & Recreation
50 West Kellogg Boulevard, Suite 840
St. Paul, MN 55102
651/266-6400
www.stpaul.gov

MINNESOTA HIKING CLUBS

Meet new people and enjoy the outdoors with your friends.

Minnesota Hiking and Backpacking Clubs
www.hikingandbackpacking.com/minnesotaclubs.html

Minnesota Rovers Outdoors Club
www.mnrovers.org

Minnesota State Park Hiking Club
www.dnr.state.mn.us

Outdoors Club
www.outdoorsclub.org

Sierra Club, Minnesota North Star Chapter
www.sierraclub.org/minnesota

OTHER SOURCES FOR MINNESOTA OUTDOOR INFORMATION

Bird-Watching Clubs
www.zumbrovalleyaudubon.org

Hiking Gear and Trail Reviews
wwww.rei.com
www.backcountry.com

Minnesota Speleological Survey
www.sites.google.com/site/msscaves

Minnesota Wildflower Information
www.dnr.state.mn.us/wildflowers

Index

Acknowledgments

Minnesota is my home state, and a place I will always call home. Writing and revising this guide has given me the opportunity to observe and enjoy the places I love in a unique and rewarding way.

I would like to thank my wife, Kerstin, for her encouragement; my editor, Rachel Feldman, for her direction; and everyone in my life who has helped me develop a love for the outdoors.

Special thanks to the Minnesota State Park system for granting me access to the parks and trails, and to the citizens of Minnesota for preserving our outdoor spaces.

MOON NATIONAL PARKS

ACADIA
NATIONAL PARK
HILARY NANGLE

ARCHES &
CANYONLANDS
NATIONAL PARKS
W. C. McRAE & JUDY JEWELL

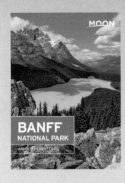

BANFF
NATIONAL PARK
ANDREW HEMPSTEAD

DEATH VALLEY
NATIONAL PARK
JENNA BLOUGH

GLACIER
NATIONAL PARK
BECKY LOMAX

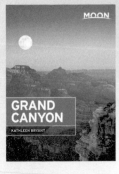

GRAND
CANYON
KATHLEEN BRYANT

GREAT SMOKY
MOUNTAINS
NATIONAL PARK
JASON FRYE

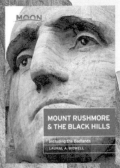

MOUNT RUSHMORE
& THE BLACK HILLS
Including the Badlands
LAURAL A. BIDWELL

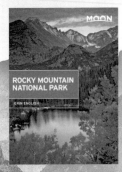

ROCKY MOUNTAIN
NATIONAL PARK
ERIN ENGLISH

In these books:

- Full coverage of gateway cities and towns
- Itineraries from one day to multiple weeks
- Advice on where to stay (or camp) in and around the parks

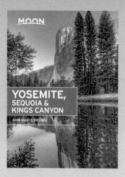

MOON ROAD TRIP GUIDES

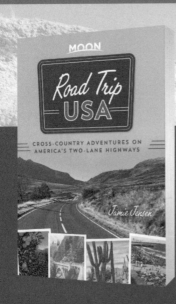

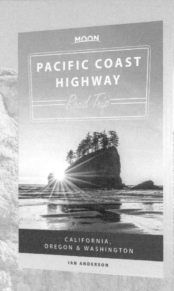

Road Trip USA

Criss-cross the country on America's classic two-lane highways with the newest edition of *Road Trip USA!*

Packed with over 125 detailed driving maps (covering more than 35,000 miles), colorful photos and illustrations of America both then and now, and mile-by-mile highlights

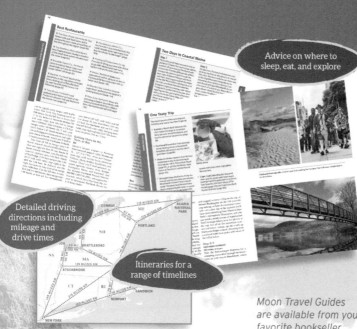

Advice on where to sleep, eat, and explore

Detailed driving directions including mileage and drive times

Itineraries for a range of timelines

Moon Travel Guides are available from your favorite bookseller.

More Guides & Getaways

CHICAGO

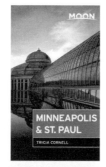

MINNEAPOLIS & ST. PAUL

TRICIA CORNELL

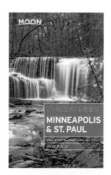

MINNEAPOLIS & ST. PAUL

MICHIGAN

PAUL VACHON

MICHIGAN'S UPPER PENINSULA

PAUL VACHON

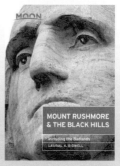

MOUNT RUSHMORE & THE BLACK HILLS

including the Badlands

LAURAL A. BIDWELL

ROUTE 66

MIDPOINT CAFE

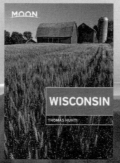

WISCONSIN

THOMAS HUHTI

WISCONSIN'S DOOR COUNTY

THOMAS HUHTI

MOON 75 GREAT HIKES
MINNEAPOLIS & ST. PAUL

Avalon Travel
Hachette Book Group
1700 Fourth Street
Berkeley, CA 94710, USA
www.moon.com

Editor: Rachel Feldman
Series Manager: Sabrina Young
Copy Editor: Linda Cabasin
Production and Graphics Coordinator:
   Suzanne Albertson
Cover Design: Faceout Studios, Charles Brock
Moon Logo: Tim McGrath
Map Editor: Kat Bennett
Cartographer: Larissa Gatt
Indexer: Greg Jewett

ISBN-13: 978-1-64049-184-7

Printing History
1st Edition – July 2018
5 4 3 2 1

Front cover photo: Hidden Falls in Nerstrand-Big
   Woods State Park, Minnesota © John Stocker
   | Dreamstime
Title page photo: © Jake Kulju
Photos on pages 3-5: © Jake Kulju
Back cover photo: Hiking in the morning mist
   © Viorel Dudau | Dreamstime

Printed in Canada by Friesens

ABOUT THE AUTHOR

Jake Kulju

© SHAUN LIBOON

Jake Kulju has been hiking Minnesota trails ever since he could tie the laces on a pair of hiking boots. He's spent his whole life unearthing morel mushrooms, watching red-tailed hawks soaring over meadows, and hunting for crawfish on the banks of the Mississippi River. He hardly lets the dust settle on a trail before heading out for another hike.

Jake currently lives in St. Paul, where he has built a vocation around his love for the great northwoods. He recounts his outdoor adventures in monthly columns for *Outdoor Traditions* magazine and the *Voyageur Press*. Find more of his work at jakekulju.com.

About Moon

Moon travel guidebooks are published by Avalon Travel, an imprint of Perseus Books, a Hachette Book Group company. Moon was founded by Bill Dalton in 1973 with the publication of his own legendary *Indonesia Handbook,* soon followed by Handbooks to Japan, the South Pacific, and Arizona. Today, Moon specializes in guides to the United States, while also publishing books on Canada, Mexico, the Caribbean, Latin America, Europe, Asia, and the Pacific. The Avalon Travel office is in Berkeley, California, and our authors call places all over the world home.

Your Adventure Starts Here

Looking for some fresh air and a brief escape from city life? Outdoors expert Jake k...up and down trails w... Cities metro area, Brainerd Lakes and the Mississippi River Valley, the St. Croix River Valley, and the Minnesota River Valley—all within two hours of Minneapolis and St. Paul.

Features include:

- Descriptions of trails ranging ...ort, flat routes suitable ...lies to daylong, steep ...ks ...or more advanced hikers

- Best Hikes lists, such as Best Views and Best for Waterfalls

- Detailed directions to each trailhead

- An easy-to-use map for each trail with point-by-point navigation

- Options to extend or shorten each hike

FIRST EDITION   AVALON TRAV...
An imprint of Perseus Books
A Hachette Book Group company

PUBLISHED JULY 2018
TRAVEL   US $17.99 CAN $23...
ISBN 978-1-64049-184-7

51799

9 781640 491847

MOON.COM 🇫 🐦 📌 📷